SECOND EDITION

PRAYER STRATEGY: GOD'S PROVOCATIVE PLAN FOR WEALTH

BY
ANN BANDINI

PRESS

Dear Jo

Jeremiah 33:3

Psalm 51:10

Romans 12:1

Book Testimonials:

D ue to the international attention given to the profound message written in _Prayer Strategy: Gods Provocative Plan for Wealth,_ it has been expanded and updated into this Second Edition to bring you the empowering roadmap necessary to apply prayerful kingdom insights for financial leadership.

Please make note, that intimacy with God and a life of prayer is crucial for days ahead in the financial marketplaces of the world. Please enjoy many of the testimonies from around the world.

One of the awesome intercessors called to my ministry (also Anne) was told she had to have your book and she passed it on to me. The Father has called me to structure and fund end-time ministries and via revelation has revealed the whole strategy over the past 5 years. He told me He was sending interces-

sors and I have two incredible women praying for the launch of this ministry placed with me. My wife Cate was supernaturally brought to me by Jesus (this is our 2nd marriage) and we have laid everything down before Him so as to be able to run the full race in obedience.

Your chapter on "how to execute a strategic prayer plan" is the final equipping I need as an end time predestined king, sitting on my authority throne with my Queen Esther and as high priest of my household. Thank you for your great diligence in compiling this book and I thank the Father for delivering it into my hands. I come alive when I read your warning on the back of your book. This describes the four of us (Cate & I, Lyn & Anne) who are at the heart of this ministry. We are desperate, hungry and tenacious...

Blessings,
Anthony Adams
South Africa

Thank you, it is so important! I don't have words enough to describe the importance for me having (your book) and meeting you even though we didn't talk much. I was with my husband Mats and I was the one working with film, television, radio and newspaper, Sofia. I told you that you would hear from me when I had read your book. Well I am still reading it, over and over again, chapter after chapter. I have not come to the end yet because of the importance of "living the message."

Love,
Sofia Dernönd, DACAPO Media
Sweden

I really praise God for the heart to heart connection he gave us at Altensteig. Thanks for your book too. I devoured it at Frankfurt, Airport as I transitioned to fly back. But it's one of those books that needs chewing over more deliberately. I sense a drawing to have you come and minister among our intercessors and business people. The Lord literally thrust me into the marketplace ministry last year. What a gruesome 12 months it has been.

Thankfully, the Lord is bringing in my life people like you to whom He has already entrusted exciting kingdom entrepreneurial revelation truths. The moment I talked to you at The Traube Berneck (hotel), I sensed a wonderful connection. I praise the Lord so much. We do not have to struggle alone.

I look forward to what the Lord has for Zambia through you,

Derek Mutungu
ICCC President Zambia, Africa

I have read until now two thirds of your book and must confess, that your book was of a greater blessing than I expected. Do you know the time when your book will be translated into German or French? Is it available in bookshops somewhere? Looking forward to hearing from you. I greet and bless you in the mighty and holy name of our Jeschua HaMaschiach.

Yours,
Hans Peter & Brigitta Ersham
Switzerland

There is a great need within me to write a few words of thanks and appreciation to you after reading your book Charles Bosomworth was so kind to make available to me.
To be honest your book has given me satisfaction and encouragement of many of my thoughts and actions, but at the same time it has deeply disturbed me as it uncovered and laid bare many neglected areas in my life, which now after reading your book I'm inspired to correct and I'm praying that the Lord will guide me to find the way to his heart and his Kingdom.
The effect of reading your book dear Ann are so strong that I'm surprised finding myself reading the Bible, under the kind guidance of my friend Brian Bosomworth, Charles' father, which before I always found to difficult to read and even more difficult to understand. But in

mysterious way after I committed myself to earnestly read and learn from the bible, I find a desire to read, which I never had before. In the spirit of love for Jesus I greet you.

Respectfully,
Karl F. Schuller
United Kingdom

I can't tell you how many times and how much effort I took trying to just read chapter one of your book previously. I even skipped to chapter 4 and started reading chapters into a recorder. But none of it would go in. My poor son Dwayne, he was worse than me. He went up North and forgot to take the book with him. I knew this was not good. But when I opened your book on the airplane, the Holy Spirit opened up my mind and I was able to take it ALL in.

YOUR BOOK WAS THE HANDBOOK I NEEDED IN ORDER TO KNOW WHAT TO DO WHEN I GOT BACK home. Praise the Holy Name of Jesus. I was, SO, SO, SO Blessed. When I was reading your book, I no longer heard your voice, but I begin to hear the voice of God. God spoke to me directly from your book. It was amazing. I am tempted to tell Dr. Frasure that he should send everyone home from counseling with a bible and your book (smile).

Debra McClendon
California USA

Good news...your prayer for the children in the book "Prayer Strategy" is starting to show up in the life of my son Benjamin! Kurt and I pray it every day. I met with my son yesterday, and he started to share problems as divination, and astral trips...I did explain to him that it is bad spirits which play with his life, and in the name of Jesus, we have the authority to deliver him from this...he said okay, and that was it! I thank so much Jesus, He is so good!!! My daughter had so much pleasure to meet you too, and sends you a big kiss.

Now it's Kurt writing a few words:
Hello Ann, yes, it was a very great pleasure for me too to meet you. Last weekend I was teacher of 25 young people (finishing their studies at the University), and I told them about your strategy prayer book... Many good things are going on here in our Country; the Lord is "back at work...." Tonight we start a new class 'Finances on Biblical Basics' (with 20 young people from the church you visited) with the Crown Ministries program.

Big blessings from Switzerland!!
Lis and Kurt Buelman

<u>AUTHOR CONTACT INFORMATION</u>

A nn Bandini can be reached for mentoring, training and discipleship through:

- **The 5 Key Principles of Prayer for Financial Success Seminars**
- **The Team 12/12 Mentoring Program**
- **The Third Thursday Tele-classes**
- **Women's Financial Network**
- **Prayer School for Financial Leaders**

Please visit the CEO Leadership Consulting and Training Institute website for more information at:
www.ceoleadershipconsultingandtrainingin-stitute.biz

Contact via email at:
annbannmentormail@earthlink.net

Contact via email at:
CEO Leadership Consulting and Training
Institute
P.O. Box 16696
Irvine, CA 92623 USA
949 440-9812

<u>PRAYER STRATEGY: GOD'S PROVOCATIVE PLAN FOR WEALTH</u>

PRAYER: A devout petition to God; a spiritual communication with God as in supplication.

STRATEGY: The art of directing large scale military movement; a scheme to surprise the enemy; intended to destroy the enemy's war making capacity.

GOD'S: The Creator and ruler of the universe; Supreme Being.

PROVOCATIVE: To stir up, to give use: to induce or bring about.

PLAN: A design or arrangement: an outline to have in mind, or intention for a specific project or definite goal.

FOR: In favor of.

WEALTH: A great quality or store of money, property, or other riches. Plentiful amount, abundance, rich or valuable content. The state of being rich, prosperous, affluence.

CONTENTS

The Purpose of this Book:

*P*rayer Strategy: God's Provocative Plan for Wealth will challenge you to come out of mediocrity and provoke you into a life of prayer so you can obtain great wealth for God's purpose.

This book is dedicated to help you take out all the stops and press into new levels of prayer and intimacy with God. *Prayer Strategy: God's Provocative Plan for Wealth* will lay the groundwork to teach the diligent, the hungry, and the passionate—those who choose to deepen their understanding and relationship with God. The kind of provocative wealth God wants to grant you will only come by dwelling with Him in intimate fellowship in the secret place of the Most High.

You are probably familiar with the term "Information Highway" coined in the computer age where one can search the world for information and knowledge. But *Prayer Strategy: God's Provocative Plan for Wealth* will help you tap into the spiritual highway—a place of supernatural communication where you will be trained by God Himself.

The information you will receive in the secret place of the Most High transcends the natural realm, and develops you in the spiritual realm because it is orchestrated by the power of the Holy Spirit, who will lead and guide you into all truth.

God has so much to pour into you –both of His magnificent Presence and also of His abundant wealth. But to attain the kind of powerful wealth God desires to grant you, prayer is not an option. It is a mandate! The day is fast approaching when you can't continue to leave home without it!

But prayer is not only taught, it is also "caught." You must not only learn the principles of effectual prayer, you must also know how to yield to the spirit of prayer. In other words, if the wealth of the wicked is to be transferred to the righteous do you qualify and why?

Prayer Strategy: God's Provocative Plan for Wealth is for those who choose to develop an excellent spirit like Daniel. Not only did Daniel pray faithfully three times daily, but as a result, he was also exalted to the highest position in the Babylonian realm—next to the king himself.

In His life Daniel not only stood against enemy forces, but he also would not bow to the political or religious systems that prevailed against the integrity of His God. The evil one set up leaders against him and his three Hebrew companions, but Daniel's faith in God was unmovable, unshakable, and unstoppable. He trusted God to intervene in the worst situation, and because he paid the price in prayer, he passed the tests in life. And God granted him promotion, success, and wealth. Are you willing to pay the price like Daniel to pass your tests in life? ECCLESIATES 2:26 says, "that it's the sinners task to heap up wealth to give to those who are good in God's sight." Do you qualify?

Qualifying for God's provocative wealth will cost you. It will cost you to be faithful in prayer to God. You must learn prevailing faith. God is calling you, His church, to attention! He is demanding character, obedience, and sacrifice, so He can trust you when He pours out vast financial resources to fund the end-time harvest.

Blessed person, as you study. *Prayer Strategy: God's Provocative Plan for Wealth*, it is my prayer that you will never be the same. As you gain a new capacity for spiritual insight by dwelling in God's Presence, the Holy Spirit will be your Teacher, God's Spirit will build into you His ideas and release divine connections to propel you into your great destiny of wealth so you can change the course of this world for Christ. God's wealth released to you is not for self -consumption; it's for Christ's purposes and His glory.

We must be a holy people; we must sanctify our motives, repent of our sins, and become vessels of honor. God wants you to be more than superficial religious models. He is calling us into kingship – joint seating with Christ. He is beckoning us into talented leadership, earmarked by Him for provocative wealth so we can serve His servants. We must be sensitive to ministries He has assigned for us to pour our finances into. He will give us specific visions and align us to be financial supporters for those who are called to be end-time priests and, "kingdom builders." Those who sit passively on the sidelines will not qualify for God's provocative wealth, nor be able to receive it!

Stay in God's Presence so you can be empowered to release your gifts! Open yourself up and walk into the office of the giver to fulfill your great commission. People are depending on you and me. We must prepare quickly to move with God's timing to receive God's great wealth!

<u>Dedication</u>

This book is dedicated to my daughter, Desdemona Bandini, a beautiful young woman who is very precious. Precious means highly-esteemed for nonmaterial value, "dearly beloved." This is a verse from a scripture that describes my feelings for her:

I Corinthians 13:7
"Love bears up under anything and everything that comes, is ever ready to believe the best of every person, it's hopes are fadeless under all circumstances, and it endures everything (without weakening)." (Amplified Bible)

<u>Fulfilling the Vision</u>

Ezekiel 12:21-28
"And the word of the Lord came to me, saying, Son of man, what is this proverb that you have in the land of Israel, saying, The days drag on and every vision comes to nothing and is not fulfilled?

Tell them therefore, Thus, says the Lord God; I will put an end to this proverb, and they shall use it no more as a proverb in Israel. But say to them, The days are at hand and the fulfillment of every vision. For there shall be no more any false, empty, and fruitless vision or flattering divination in the house of Israel.

For I am the Lord; I will speak, and the word that I shall speak shall be performed (come to pass); it shall be no more delayed or prolonged, for in your days, O rebellious house, I will speak the word and will perform it, says the Lord God.

Again the word of the Lord came to me, saying, son of man behold, they of the house of Israel say, The vision that [Ezekiel] sees is for many days to come, and he prophesies of the times that are far off. Therefore say to them, Thus says the Lord God; There shall none of My words be deferred any more, but the word which I have spoken shall be performed, says the Lord God." (Amplified Bible)

Chapter 1

THE BENEFITS OF MINISTERING FIRST TO THE LORD

EXODUS 20:1-3
And God spoke all these words, saying: "I am the Lord your God, who brought you out of the land of Egypt, out of the house of bondage. "You shall have no other gods before Me."

Have you ever wondered about the importance of God's very first commandment? It must be significant for God to list this commandment before all others or He would not have placed it in that order. God is a God of order, and He placed this foremost commandment first for a reason. He is allowing us to receive this instruction of seeking to deepen our personal understanding for tremendous blessings and knowledge through communication with the divine nature. We begin a journey to walk in bridal intimacy. God knows that if your priorities are right, then everything else in your life will fall into place. He knows if you obey His first commandment, blessings will follow, intimacy will follow, and protection will follow.

God's first commandment is this:

Exodus 20:3
You shall have no other gods before Me.

God not only commands His children to have no other God's before Him, but He also warns us what can happen to those who disobey this command. God first gives us the instruction, and then tells us why we need to follow it. We can see the consequence of disobedience in another scripture that parallels the First Commandment:

Deuteronomy 6:13-15
You shall fear the Lord your God and serve Him, and shall take oaths in His name. You shall not go after other gods, the gods of the peoples who are all around you (for the Lord your God is a jealous God among you), lest the anger of the Lord your God be aroused against you and destroy you from the face of the earth.

The reason God commands His people to love Him before anything else is that He *must be first in our lives* so we can be a true success. God will only ask us to do things that will ultimately benefit us. That is why God draws us into an intimate understanding of the Lordship of Jesus Christ today.

Jesus has been calling Christians—wooing us to deepen our relationship with Him. He wants us to open ourselves up to a more intimate understanding of Him so we can come to a place of intimacy, acknowledging His Lordship. God is drawing us to Him because He knows that in the absolute sense, we will succeed no matter what happens and triumph over any trials or difficulties we may experience if we are first lovers of God.

To Love God is *to minister to God*. When we give ourselves completely to Him and to His service, we are ministering to God. We must present ourselves, our attention, our whole being in total surrender to God. Our surrender allows God a place of supreme authority and total submission in our lives. It is done willingly and longingly!

Initially we come into the Kingdom of God by surrendering to Him and repenting of our sins and by allowing God to change our ungodly nature (2 Corinthians 5:17). He shows us our personal iniquity and separation and draws us to respond to the changes. We must understand that God longs for us to come to Him in total dependence and abandon ourselves to His supreme Lordship.

The word "lordship" implies authority, influence, and power. Lordship means being master or ruler. So when we speak of the "Lordship of Jesus Christ" we are talking about giving the reigns of our lives to Him—allowing the Lord to be our leader in all areas. By allowing Jesus to influence even the intimate areas of our lives; for example, all our ideas, attitudes and plans, He can, in turn, give us direction and release His purpose in our lives. He wants to reveal mysteries as we seek to be hidden in Him. Our destinies are tangibly revealed!

We were created to minister to the Lord, and to enjoy fellowship and relationship with our God. That is why He is now drawing His Bride, the Christian Church, to a place of greater submission to Him. We become fervent worshippers and praisers of God. And as we deeply and fervently minister to the Lord in worship extending to Him our praise and adoration, we experience an expression of joy that satisfies our hearts.

The human soul was designed to experience God's love by the revelation of His Spirit. Intimate communion with God is the most enjoyable and pleasurable experience available to mankind. We were created to love God passionately with our whole heart!

We have been created to be passionate lovers of God! It is stirring and compelling when we learn to be responsive to this passion.

It is not just that we *should* love God passionately, but we *must* in order to function the right way. When we discover the precious truth of a sweet relationship with God, we become discontented to just live a life of mediocrity. We have an unquenchable longing to experience the deepest love extended to us by our Lord and Savior Jesus Christ.

As we pray and worship the Lord, we become His fragrance in the earth. We are the only aroma of Christ to the world. We take on the perfume of being loved by Him alone. When we come before Jesus and minister to Him above everything or everyone else in our lives, a divine exchange occurs—the fragrance of His love permeates our being.

2 Corinthians 2:14-16
Now thanks be to God who always leads us in triumph in Christ, and through us DIFFUSES THE FRAGRANCE OF HIS KNOWLEDGE in every place. For we are to God THE FRAGRANCE OF CHRIST among those who are being saved and among those who are perishing. To the one we are THE AROMA OF DEATH TO DEATH, and to THE OTHER THE AROMA OF LIFE TO LIFE.

The transforming fragrance of Christ's love is like a beautiful perfume or the fresh scent of aromatic flowers that enraptures us all. Just as it is uplifting and pleasing to experience the pleasure of an aromatic scent wafting in the air, so too it is uplifting and pleasing to experience the fragrance of Christ's love. We experience the drawing to a lovely fragrance in one another both naturally and spiritually.

The exchange we receive when we minister to the Lord affects our very environment and the places God sends us to throughout the day. The fragrance of God's anointing upon us is a tangible substance.

This is vital because we are seen and read by people all around us. It is Christ's fragrance in us that draws and compels people toward us.

The Bible tells us that Christ's love transforms us:

Ephesians 5:2
And walk in love, as Christ also has loved us and given Himself for us, an offering and a sacrifice to God for A SWEET-SMELLING AROMA.

We exchange our time by being obedient to minister to the Lord, and without our knowledge God places His anointing on our lives to embrace the needs of those around us throughout the day. Others may not understand it, but they will be compelled to seek us for answers—just because of the anointing we carry upon our lives.

Actually the greatest way we can value our time is to seek God each day!

By allowing the daily discipline of ministering to the Lord to supersede all other demands we will fall deeper and deeper in love with our Savior. Soon we will ache to run to God to rekindle and reunite with Him in intimate fellowship.

This divine bonding with God—us in Him and Him in us—is an investment to all those around us in a lost and dying world. With the anointing of God's divine fragrance upon us we won't even need to work at evangelism! As we become deeper lovers of God, we will be so in tune with those around us that the fruit of the spirit will constantly flow out from us to change them.

Let's examine what the Bible tells us about the fruit of the spirit and how it manifests in our lives as we spend time ministering to the Lord. The Bible lists the fruit of the spirit:

GALATIANS 5:22, 23
But the fruit of the Spirit is Love, joy, peace, long-suffering, kindness, goodness, faithfulness, gentleness, self-control. Against such there is no law.

Now let's take a closer look at each fruit of the spirit individually. Webster's dictionary gives the following descriptions of the words we know as the fruits of the spirit:

Love
A profoundly tender, passionate affection for another person. A feeling of warm personal attachment or deep affection. A person toward whom love is felt. Affectionate concern for the well being of others; love of one's neighbor.

Joy
A feeling or state of great delight or happiness caused by something exceptionally good or satisfying. Keen pleasure; elation. A source of keen pleasure or delight. The expression or display of glad feeling. To feel joy, be glad, rejoice.

Gladness
Feeling joy, delight, or pleasure. Accompanied by or causing joy or pleasure. Characterized by showing cheerfulness.

Peace
Freedom from anxiety, annoyance or other mental disturbance. Peace of mind. State of tranquility.

Temperance
Self control, moderation, or self-restraint. A Habit of the mind that allows one to practice restraint, patience; a disposition of being even tempered.

Forbearance /Kindness
Of good or benevolent disposition; as a compassionate person. Having shown or *possessing* benevolence. Kind words considerate or helpful, humane, mild, gentle, benign, clement, loving, affectionate.

Goodness
A state or quality of being good; moral excellence, virtue, kindness, generosity. The best or most valuable part of anything. Morality or virtue refers to quality of character or conduct that entitles the possessor to approval and esteem. Goodness is the simple word for the general quality recognized as an inherent part of one's character. Virtue suggests goodness that is concisely or steadily maintained often in spite of temptation or evil influence.

Faithfulness
Steady in allegiance or affection. Stability, depend-ability, and devotion. Faithfulness implies enduring fidelity to what is bound by a pledge, duty, or obliga-tion, for example, a faithful friend. Suggests lack of change in affections or loyalties.

Gentleness
Not severe, rough, or violent. Mild, polite, refined, courteous.

Meekness
Humble, patient, docile, especially under provoca-tion from others; gentle, kind.

Humility
Modest opinion of one's own importance or rank: meekness.

Self-control
Restraint of oneself or one's actions or feelings.

As we allow the fruit of the spirit to grow and develop in our lives, our character is transformed. Our love relationship with the Lord Jesus Christ produces the fruit of the spirit in our lives. The fruit of the spirit is revealed through us as we minister to the Lord. Nothing can dismantle demonic activity faster than operating in the fruit of the spirit!

As we spend time ministering to the Lord and grow in the fruit of the spirit, we repel opposition. Abrasive opposition from the world that normally provokes, attacks, disagrees and degrades us—acting as sandpaper against us—is diffused by the peace flowing from the fruit of the spirit in our lives.

By ministering to the Lord we are insulated from the contamination and unclean activities of the world trying to influence our environments. As we grow in the fruit of the spirit, God protects us from worldly pollutants that try to attach themselves to us.

Ministering to the Lord also gives us greater discernment about that which is not appropriate for our spiritual growth. As we spend time with the Lord we gain a greater discernment about guarding our sensory gates—guarding our eyes, ears, nose and mouth—from the world's contamination.

We must guard the holy and sacred exchange we receive from our love relationship with God. Also, as we develop our love relationship with God, God will reveal hidden or unexposed sin.

As we seek God, we learn to protect ourselves from opposing assignments by covering ourselves with the glory of God and knowing that we are washed in the blood of Jesus and have the protection from the heavenly realm by wearing Gods armor. Also, when we minister to the Lord we learn about the protection of angels on assignment and our covenant rights of protection (Psalm. 91). Angels are empowered and dispatched as we speak forth God's Word. We need their intervention daily. They marshal His plans as we depend on our relationship with them in our daily sphere of influence. These are there to do our bidding based on the power of Gods words.

Psalm 103:20

Bless the Lord, you His angels, who excel in strength, who do His word, heeding the voice of His word.

Hebrews 1:14

Are they not all ministering spirits sent forth to minister for those who will inherent salvation.

ABIDING IN HIM ALONE

By spending time in God's presence, we begin to develop a place of habitation. We make a home in His presence. The Bible calls this abiding in His presence. To abide in God's presence is the same as to dwell or reside in God. It is accepting all that God is without opposition. It is the peace and safety from daily stresses.

When we abide in God, we yield completely to Him. We endure in Him—in the secret place of the Most High by His Spirit—no matter what the cost. Abiding in God develops staying power to keep connected to the Lord, no matter what!

JOHN 15:7-10

If you abide in Me, and My words abide in you, you will ask what you desire, and it shall be done for you. By this My Father is glorified, that you bear much fruit; so you will be My disciples.

As the Father loved Me, I also have loved you; abide in My love.

If you keep My commandments, you will abide in My love, just as I have kept My Father's commandments and abide in His love.

By God's engrafting us into Him, we have taken our residence in the Lord because we choose to abide in Him. As we reside in the power of His Word, we become immersed in God's protective power. It is by this attached network—us in God and God in us— that our prayers and petitions before the throne of God ensure enduring success.

We must yield to the discipline of coming before the Lord! Entering into this new dominion allows us the ability to become one with Him as we offer Him our pure devotion and adoration.

Becoming one with the Lord in worship is the most powerful form of warfare!

Honoring our Master and Maker with our worship prepares us to be carriers of God's glory. By this, we establish a wonderful love relationship of our own choosing. Jesus is our priority, opening the pathway to extend His love to others because through Him we become the outflow of God's love to others.

As yielded vessels we allow the Lord to take possession of us—our highest calling!

SEEKING HIS FACE AND NOT HIS HAND

Abiding and residing in habitation are established by our daily surrender. Everyday we experience a fresh new opportunity to establish and connect with our Redeemer. Each morning I am swept into praise and worship by the following words which have been taken from the Kim Clement song "FACE TO FACE"

With these words I begin to enter into the Lord's magnificent presence. Won't you allow the anointing of these lyrics to empower your spirit as you ponder them:

"Hold me Lord. It's in your embrace. Bid me welcome to the Secret Place.

There is nothing more that I desire than to come forth before Your sweet face. Because here in, Your presence time stands still. My spirit soars to know Your will. Won't You transform me Lord into who You see in me. How I treasure Your sweet intimacy. Face to face, You and I, We shall see each other as we really are, Face to Face. So here I am in Your Secret Place. I'm attracted to Your holiness, and through Your grace You rain down unmerited favor and Your promises. Lord, I draw near without fear, knowing the truth sets me free. So help me worship You in sweet intimacy. Face to face, face to face….. I have opened the heavens for you."

While meditating on these words they become very real to me. You see, the Lord is not looking for talent, He's looking for faithfulness. We are very undeserving when we come before Him. It's by His mercy alone that we are compelled to attain a place of humility and separation from our own lusts, desires and carnal distractions. By this demonstration of humility we choose to desperately seek Him.

Intimacy with the Lord when properly developed will far exceed our desires just for provision.

We need to seek His face and not His hand. As our fleshly desires begin to fade in comparison, we will begin to lay down our own good works. It's at this time the Lord begins to observe our commitment to Him and to His service. Many of us have been deceived by presumption, yet we think we serve Him. Are we really convicted of our desperate need for Him daily? Is our prayer life convicting us of how self-sufficient we really are? It's in His presence that we see His holy sustaining power. Do you live each day as if it's your last? If you seek Him you will find Him. Is your heart humble, hungry and desperate for God? In your prayer life is there more passion for the people (the souls) in your sphere of influence than just earning a living? Is making money or having an abundance of financial prosperity and your right to money consuming your thoughts? As we appropriate our covenant of prosperity and our gift to be stewards of the acquisition of wealth, do we not desire to see souls in eternity with greater passion than our own personal material prosperity and blessings?

Are our thoughts in our daily routine about the "appointments," the "deals," the "meetings," the "connections" and the "positioning?" Have you asked your teacher, your guide, the Holy Spirit for the details of each day before you launch out? Do you carry the anointed fragrance of the Lord Jesus Christ into the marketplace? Are the people in your sphere of influence *so attracted by "Him" in your life* that, they seek you out for counsel about their needs?

Can they draw on what the Holy Spirit and the Lord Jesus has imparted to you for that day because you have valued His directives each morning? Are the divine details He gave you exactly what each person you encounter needs on each separate occasion that day? In His awesome sustaining presence is holiness amplified each day?

2 TIMOTHY 2:1-2

"So you, my son, be strong (strengthened inwardly) in grace (spiritual blessings) that is to be found only in Christ Jesus. And the instructions which you have heard from me along with many witnesses, transmit and entrust (as a deposit) to reliable and fruitful men who will be competent and qualified to teach others also." (Amplified Bible)

2 TIMOTHY 2:7

"Think over these sayings, understand them and grasp their application. For the Lord will grant full insight and understanding in everything." (Amplified Bible)

Chapter 2

REACHING HIGHER
LEVELS IN PRAYER

PRAYER AT A HIGHER LEVEL

*W*hat do we mean by levels of prayer? And how do Christians advance from one level of prayer to the next? First of all, levels of prayer can be measured by the heart. Prayers sincerely prayed from the heart develop a deeper intimacy *with God* and reveal a spirit of truth—present truth which is being released in greater measure today for this season in God's plan. Prayers prayed from the heart bring forth new and deep revelations of what the spirit of God is saying today.

In order to advance from one level of prayer to higher levels, increasing in intimacy with God and His revelations, we must pause from our busy agendas and our familiar schedules. We must be willing to allow the Holy Spirit to blow fresh life into our prayer times. We must allow God to disrupt our complacency.

A shaking has been happening in the Body of Christ as we have transitioned from the church age into the kingdom age. We have experienced this to bring us into the deeper things of God. We have to leave behind first principles and move onto strong meat. The shaking comes to trumpet a new sound being released so that we can move into the new seasons and continue to become desperate for Gods new order.

In the Body of Christ there has been a mixture of old traditions and religious mindsets. The problem is the Holy Spirit has been contained in our old traditions and religious thinking. In order for this containment to be broken open, there must be a renewed separation to holiness and sanctification brought on by humility and brokenness. We now know that this shift has been ordered by God as we have stepped into the third millennium. It was dislodging us over a ten to fifteen year period but now we have arrived in this new season.

So in order to reach higher levels of prayer, we must learn to flow with the Holy Spirit, no longer planning our own agendas. Instead, we must learn to bow in the Presence of His Majesty in awesome reverence, repentance, and humility. Are we waiting and willing to allow death to self, both personally and corporately to permeate our being?

It is time to allow the Holy Spirit to fully reign without fear of what it might cost us. We must be willing to lay down everything for God, hearing Him accurately, and allowing Him to give us new direction. Then we must move and act on what He says. By following these principles in this season, new life and resurrection will come!

Believers can reach higher levels in prayer if we will pay the price to become more intimately acquainted with God. The sifting that comes from paying this price will refine us, bringing all the dross in our lives to the top.

To go deeper in prayer requires that every hidden agenda, every unclean thing, every inflated ego, all spirits of pride must be skimmed off like dross in a refiner's pot. All manifestations which oppose the preparation of God's coming glory must be set aside so the Body of Christ can reach new levels in God.

On our own, we are incapable of standing in the glory of God until we are first separated into a holy intimacy with God. This is brought about by affirmation from God alone. Because of our own insufficiency, we must obediently give ourselves over to Him and His directives so He can be our sufficiency (2 Corinthians 3:5). God alone must be our sufficiency! He longs for us to come and sit at His feet so He can instruct us.

God has waited so long for this hour! We can no longer continue without this fresh, daily out-pouring of His Spirit, first on a personal level and then on a corporate level. God allows the shaking so we can never get into presumption.

The Body of Christ must keep current with the moves of God and come out of our comfort zones. We must ask ourselves this question: Are we looking for comfort zones? Clearly the whole earth is groaning for the redemption of the sons of man. There can be nothing left but ridding ourselves of our comfort it is not an option—it's imperative if we are to reach our highest calling and achievements ordained by Him! Comfort is a western mindset and prevents us from attaining the high calling of God. We must step out of this in faith and obedience!

Are we willing to pay the price to reach higher levels in God? It may cost much, but ultimately it pays abundantly! Are we willing to be yielded vessels to usher in the glory of God? His glory is filling the earth today!

The Bible tells us how much God longs for the Body of Christ to come forth out of our western mind set and comfort so we can reach higher levels in Him.

Romans 8:19
For the earnest expectation of the creation eagerly waits for the revealing of the sons of God.

God's Word makes a clear distinction between those who are willing to pay the price to reach new levels in Him and those who are not.

Romans 8:5, 6
For those who live according to the flesh set their minds on things of the flesh, but those who live according to the Spirit the things of the Spirit. For to be carnally minded is

death, but to be spiritually minded is life and peace.

In other words, the Bible says those who are willing to pay the price to reach new levels in God live according to the Spirit. That brings life and peace! But the Bible says those who are not willing to pay the price in God live according to the flesh. They are called carnally minded Christians, and that leads only to death and dead works. The stakes are high today. We are experiencing challenges like never before. Our faith is being tested to the max. We didn't sign up for much of what we have had to live through.

One of the most important things for the Body of Christ to remember as we strive to reach higher levels in God is to not allow other demands to steal our focus. For example, when we hear and know what the Holy Spirit is saying, then it is time to pray—and birth God's plan in the Spirit. Answers to prayer must first be birthed in the Spirit, pressing all the way through until we are released and break-through occurs.

God's plan must first come by personal revelation. Until we receive a personal revelation by the Spirit of God, God's plan will not be able to have its impact in our lives! Just as the gospel of salvation brought an awesome understanding of redemption, so too the Holy Spirit increases our capacity in an awesome measure to discern truth in this hour as we stand in the understanding of gospel of the kingdom.

Another very important thing to remember as you reach higher levels in God is to safeguard revelations in the Spirit. Whenever God reveals part of His plan for our lives, we must not share mysteries and secrets with others, or release too much information about it in advance of the release. What God tells us is sacred and holy, and we should release it only to those discriminating and circumspect people who are in proper alignment with our vision. They must be people who are sent by God who are loyal and trustworthy. Only in prayer can we discern this.

Therefore, hearing God's plan, safeguarding it, sharing it only with loyal and discriminating people who are in proper alignment with your vision will promote liberty as God's plan is manifested.

Once this insight or revelation of the Holy Spirit is ready to be entrusted to others, it should only be shared with a select few for prayer and birthing in the Spirit. We must safeguard the secrets we receive from on High! Only trusted and appointed intercessors should help birth out God's secrets.

Learn to be of few words until the appointed time of release comes to share God's plan. Carry things and ponder them deeply. As one moves deeper in relationship with God, we must have a revelation of prayer that reveals the unknown mysteries and throne room experiences!

As shifting in the spirit realm comes, we must learn to hear the Holy Spirit moment by moment. We must exercise our heavenly language which is the evidence of the Holy Spirits power flowing out of us in abundance, and use the anointed authority of this gift of tongues to exercise our inner vibrant man. God's Word exhorts us to boldly exercise the inner man of the spirit.

Jude 20
But you, beloved, building yourselves up in your most holy faith, praying in the Holy Spirit.

Exercise the gift of praying in the Holy Spirit a minimum of at least one hour a day to reach deeper levels in prayer. This baptism of the Holy Spirit moves us into a place of spiritual authority, and as exercised takes residence in us to be praying at all times. Find the way that suits you best to pray in the Spirit.

For example, I find that it's easiest to pray like this as I am walking daily. I enjoy praying and walking at least one and a half hours every day. This brings me a great deal of spiritual liberty and excitement. I also find that when I drive alone, I can pray very strongly in my heavenly language. Many times I feel great breakthroughs.

This develops a great diversity in your prayer language, and it is a powerful tool. You may pray out many dialects as you develop in the Spirit by constantly praying in tongues. My prayer languages are very diverse, and I feel I am touching nations in places that I don't understand, but yet feel that God is touching my needs and the needs of others! (1 Corinthians 12:10; 14:2).

Romans 8:26, 27
Likewise the Spirit also helps in our weaknesses. For we do not know what we should pray for as we ought; but the Spirit Himself makes intercession for us with groanings which cannot be uttered.

Now He who searches the hearts knows what the mind of the Spirit is, because He makes intercession for the saints according to the will of God.

The Holy Spirit takes our weak prayers and makes them effective. This explains how the Spirit helps us in our prayer. Our cries, tears, and other expressions of our heart and spirit are taken by the Holy Spirit and made into effectual intercession before the throne of God. We respond and cry out or are compelled to weep!

The word "effectual" means capable of producing an adequate, intended effect. Our prayer becomes a valid, binding agreement with God! Our prayers produce what our covenant agreement with God has already given us. Praying in covenant agreement with God is our inherited right.

To reach high levels in prayer prune back dead works! Cut off old, dead branches—everything that represents dead works! That means we must go through a time of pruning in God. Allow fresh, new and vigorous life-giving, life-bearing sustaining power—the anointing—to produce a new move and wave of the Holy Spirit! This is not an agenda from our mind, but a new, fresh revelation of our heart!

It is circumcising our hearts! This kind of prayer is prayed by revelation of the Holy Spirit.

Jesus tells us how to reach higher levels in prayer. It's by _praying always_!

Luke 18:1
Also [Jesus] told them a parable to the effect that they ought always to pray and not to turn coward (faint, lose heart, and give up).
(Amplified Bible)

Following Jesus' instructions will encourage steadfastness in prayer and guard against discouragement as we await the return of our precious Savior. We need to please Jesus in our prayer life because He's the One we highly esteem as our dear and beloved Lord.

Jesus also tells us to listen to the Holy Spirit's instruction.

Revelation 2:17
He who has an ear, let him hear WHAT THE SPIRIT HAS TO SAY to the churches. To him who overcomes I will give some of the hidden manna to eat. And I will give him a white stone, and on the stone a new name written which no one knows except him who receives it.

Those of you who are business people especially need to develop your spiritual ears so you can reach higher levels in prayer, for you have a divine commission to fund the end-time harvest. Listen to what the Spirit is saying to you regarding making money to build God's Kingdom!

The wise believer takes time to listen with spiritual hearing to what God is saying. This is much needed today. One who hears and follows the voice of the Holy Spirit does not need to fear. Rather, he will walk in Jesus' requirements and grow in the Spirit.

Exodus 16:31-36

And the house of Israel called its name Manna. And it was like white coriander seed, and the taste of it was like wafers made with honey.

Then Moses said, "This is the thing which the Lord has commanded: 'Fill an omer with it, to be kept for your generations, that they may see the bread with which I fed you in the wilderness, when I brought you out of the land of Egypt.'"

And Moses said to Aaron, "Take a pot and put an omer of manna in it, and lay it up before the Lord, to be kept for your generations." As the Lord commanded Moses, so Aaron laid it up before the Testimony, to be kept. And the children of Israel ate manna for forty years, until they came to an inhabited land; they ate manna until they came to the border of the land of Canaan.

Our understanding of God's covenant provisions and supernatural abilities draws us to seek Him more deeply in prayer so His revelations and impartations can impact our destiny. We must have an accurate understanding of our covenant rights, because if we do not know what belongs to us, how can we appropriate it? Therefore, we must first hide ourselves away in God so we can overcome obstacles; overcome much and receive God's covenant provisions.

Revelation 3:12,13
"He who overcomes, I will make him a pillar in the temple of My God, and he shall go out no more. I will write on him the name of My God and the name of the city of My God, the New Jerusalem, which comes down out of heaven from My God. And I will write on him My new name. "He who has an ear, let him hear what the Spirit says to the churches."

The Lord will honor His faithful ones permanently by inscribing on them the name of God. This inscription, given to overcomers, indicates identification and possession by God. Special stones were also used as tokens for various purposes such as rewards.

These scriptures show us the outcome of allowing God to take us to higher levels in prayer. And if overcomers will press through in prayer, God will not only give them manna, Spiritual Bread, but He will also give them natural bread. He gifts overcomers with His signature and endorses our endeavors.

Our understanding of God's covenant provisions and supernatural abilities draws us to seek Him more deeply in prayer so His revelations and impartations can change our destiny.

And as we continue to press deeply into Gods heart in all matters, He will in turn continue to bless us with many reveled facets of Himself, pouring out revelations and insights about His plan for our lives. He will show us how we can achieve our complete destiny in Him!

Chapter 3

PURSUING INTIMACY
WITH GOD

It is most necessary to understand how to develop a daily "appointed time" spent seeking God.

Our flesh wants to keep us busy, distracted, or sometime we just get too lazy. We need to practice discipline, it is imperative in the pursuit of God. But many times when God wants our attention focused on Him alone everything starts to close down around us. With so many choices vying for our time, when we are shocked or alerted to make that choice, it may start during a time we experience difficulty or crises.

God will begin to cut away every distraction so we won't go around the mountain again and again. Instead, He will lead us on the straight path to Him.

However, in the pursuit of God, mankind needs to learn some basic instruction. So many of us came to God out of desperation; it may have been because God wouldn't let anything else work for us. Everything around us was placed there to bring us to our knees, so we would bow before Him.

You see, most people who live a fast-paced life find it difficult to understand the need to just _rest in God_. Most people are simply too busy for God. However, as never before people are becoming aware that they simply need more of Him. Many people can relate to this.

One of the most important decisions you can make, is to come completely to the end of yourself! Totally surrender everything to God each and every day of your life! Start dependant on Him! Pursue Him!

God is pursuing mankind for a deeper, more intimate revelation of Him.

We can't stay on the surface as shallow Christians and experience the longing and hunger to develop His heart for a new, more meaningful relationship and fellowship with God.

God creates within us a greater need for us to draw closer to Him so we can experience the power of His deep love, compassion, and mercy. He wants to lavishly pour out on us His instructions, plans, purposes, and details—none of which can ever be received unless we allow ourselves to be available to the wooing of His precious Holy Spirit. If we don't allow the wooing of God's Spirit, we will find His revelations to be unavailable and unattainable.

How sad God must feel when we so often blatantly dig our feet in, resisting deeper intimacy with Him. Sometimes we simply forge ahead each day without so much as acknowledging our enormous need for Him and His instruction. What we really need is a personal revelation of God's perception of our lives.

All the battles we face are minor—petty inconveniences—compared to the scope of His majestic ability to divinely intervene, providing supernatural solutions. Seeing things God's way gives us another opportunity to witness His magnificent, miracle power so we can glorify Him.

As business people, we carry a unique gifting through the diversity of our exuberant talent and the knowledge that we sustain, to walk in the anointing given to us to produce kingdom wealth. However, with these giftings and talents we can easily falter and not delegate time needed; and become distorted and draw our attention away from time well spent with God. We must control ourselves to not let this happen! We must refrain from allowing the multitudes of gifts and talents given to us by God to hinder us from this diligent discipline, or compromise His sovereign anointing which will advance us to produce kingdom resources. We must wisely choose the right priority.

As business people, we need to set our own boundaries and begin to trust that we can give God the priority with our time by seeking Him without reservation. When we surrender "ownership" to His "lordship", He will establish greater order in our daily business schedules. We will see tangible changes which could be the following examples: our production costs, operations, and staffing, and any number of things will all begin to flow without the normal conflicts and intrusions.

As business people, much of our self-esteem comes from our ability to become successful. This can be a distraction and a mistake. We need to understand our self-esteem must come from God alone. Our talents are His endowment, but used according to *His pleasure.* The substance for this will bring us enormous joy and will bring God His reward through us as we are walking in our destiny!

So let's diligently choose to separate ourselves from all distorted human weaknesses and pursue an intimate relationship with the Master.

In order to hear God, we must be in pursuit of Him with great passion. This simply means we must begin to follow Him closely. That's the only way we can attain and accomplish the goals He has for us. We will begin to experience His revelations overtaking us. He is drawing us to Him to provoke necessary changes in us!

We've been talking about pursuing intimacy with God so we can receive deeper revelation and become more successful in life and business. Now let's move from the general to the specific.

Let's create a basic form of discipline that can help us establish a daily appointment with God. The following is a six-step plan I use for establishing intimate fellowship with God on a daily basis.

Step One

- Create an appointed time to daily get alone with God and stick to it.
- Think of it as a date, a time when we won't allow anything to come between us and the Lord. Many people find early-morning prayer to be the most successful. There is little that will consume our attention at 3:00, 4:00, 5:00 or 6:00 a.m. It is a time that is quiet and peaceful and conducive to tranquility.
- This will become easier and easier as we submit to it. If necessary, fix a cup of coffee or tea to wake up. When we begin to "report in" for our appointment with God, it won't take long to get settled and enter into His Presence.

Step Two

- Choose spiritual tools for your appointment with God.
- Gather together all your "tools," including a CD or MP3 player, good worship CDs or downloads, something that you love that is compelling and something that brings the sound of heaven to change the morning atmosphere. You will need a good study Bible, a dictionary, and a concordance. I also like The Amplified Bible (so I use two Bibles) for studying God's Word.
- You will also need a note pad or prayer journal so that you can write down the things God

shares with you. Make sure you have a good-sized prayer journal so you can flow with the Spirit of God. You will enjoy journaling as it becomes familiar to you.

Step Three

- Come before the Lord in an attitude of worship.
- As I come before the Lord, I start by putting on a good worship CD or MP3. I allow the spiritual atmosphere around me to begin to change. I listen to the words of adoration coming from the worship CD (or MP3) and declare my love to the Lord. I express my desperate need for Him and begin to worship and extend my love to Him.
- As you do this yourself you will begin to feel the presence of the Holy Spirit enter into your heart and change the very atmosphere of your place of worship. You may also need a box of tissue because His Presence and power can reduce one to tears. Nothing is more precious than worshipping and waiting on the Lord.
- Continue to worship irregardless of experiencing a feeling of the tangible Presence of God immediately. For example, I often worship for at least an hour allowing the Lord to have free reign whether I start out feeling God's Presence or not. It's in this atmosphere that the Holy Spirit begins to speak to me. It's submitting to this disciple without reservation

that begins to develop consistency. Surely the Lord draws us to Him and soon we enter the tangible presence quickly.

- The way the Holy Spirit usually speaks to me is prophetically. Sometimes I am led to write what He drops into my spirit. It may even be a poetic interpretation for myself or for a specific person. I may also be led to scriptures, which allows me to use cross referenced verses, footnotes and other study tools in the different Bible translations that I use. I write out what the Lord gives me, studying out various scriptures, all the while taking notes. This is helpful to understand difficult passages. The Lord wants us to be students of His Word. He graces us with incredible knowledge as He pours forth from the Word liberally.

Step Four

- Act on what the Lord gives you.
- For example, at this point I may begin to decree out loud scriptures the Holy Spirit has given me. It is important to declare and decree God's Word. Then I may pray some of the prayers I've developed. I might also use other prayers given to me over a period of time.

Step Five

- Record anything important from the Holy Spirit in a prayer journal.

- I keep my own prayer journal as He gives me personal information at this time. I also write down what He gives me for other people so I can keep it in my files. If I am prompted, I email to the people it's for. Or I carry them for the appointed time. Remember that these exhortations, scriptures, or prophecies may be very timely for these people.

- A prayer journal is a valuable tool. It is inspiring, because you can look back and see what God has done and where you are in the plan of things. Keeping a prayer journal can also allow you to see where God has brought you from, or intervened supernaturally, or provided miraculously.

- As you pray you will begin to receive valuable instruction for that day. You may receive divine revelations in your prayer time for specific people and specific needs. God will give you valuable information, and you must be ready to impart it as the Lord delegates.

- As you are obedient to this wonderful time with the Lord, He sees it, and will begin to trust more and more information to you. It will become so exciting to know you have heard Him as He reveals things to you throughout your daily encounters with Him.

___**Step Six**___ Use points of contact to activate your faith.

- When I receive prayer requests or pictures of people, I use them as points of contact in prayer. Sometimes I feel led to lay hands on these points of contact while praying in tongues.
- This is key, because praying releases the mysteries of God into your life. Unless you pray in the Spirit you may not know how to pray for these situations or people as you ought to.

Romans 8:26,27

Likewise the Spirit also helps in our weaknesses. For we do not know what we should pray for as we ought, but the Spirit Himself makes intercession for us with groanings which cannot be uttered.

He who searches the hearts knows what the mind of the Spirit is, because He makes intercession for the saints ACCORDING TO THE WILL OF GOD.

Praying in the Spirit is praying the perfect will of God for your life or for someone else.

Another important function of using points of contact in prayer is to declare and decree the Word of God over them. Speak scriptures over these prayer requests and over people's lives.

By following these six steps in your prayer time, the power of God will become awesome to you!

It is my hope that this knowledge will assist you in your pursuit to develop a very fulfilling, intimate relationship with your wonderful Lord. I believe you will receive every answer to prayer as you build a solid foundation with God based on His Word. This foundation will assist you each and every day of your life on this earth.

As you surrender to God, you abandon yourself, giving up and relinquishing all that you are to His service. You are then ready for Him to pour supernatural ability through you to touch and transform the lives of all those around you. Let the miracles and supernatural blessings begin!

Chapter 4

OBEDIENCE IN KEEPING GOD'S LAW: A Mandate for Businesses to Create Financial Flow

I wrote this chapter for a very important reason. Frankly, I am quite amazed at people who consider themselves Christian believers, and yet lack the spiritual maturity to discern the releasing of seasons and are disobedient to God's very basic instructions. Many of these people may be gifted, because God has given them tremendously creative ideas to perform assignments that are to be established. But, because they disobey God's most basic instructions, they may ultimately fail due to their choices to disobey. We need revelation knowledge to be obedient to Gods instructions. This will come when we have committed to establishing time with God on a daily basis. The word revelation means unveiling. It cannot be a revelation until it is a *personal revelation*. It is at this juncture that we gain *ownership* by understanding that God desires to reveal all things needed to us for being progressive in what we are elected to do. Without this revelation we cannot implement our God given ideas with the success He has originally planned for us to do! One of the main secrets of all successes today is to follow closely after Gods instruction without deviation. We must discern the pure voice of the Lord in a world that clamors for many choices and demands our attention! It is imperative that we pause from our busy agendas frequently to take inventory and fine tune where we are on Gods timetable.

Many Christians know their talents and get excited by their creative ideas. However, one thing I find fascinating about many prophetically untrained people is that God speaks the prophetic words over their lives, confirming and encouraging their future success, through a prophetic voice. But many of them have been deceived into thinking they will receive an immediate manifestation of kingdom prosperity and financial releases. I think that through the last season in God we have more understanding of the *word* spoken to an individual. This is the trumpeting of God over the financial leader into the atmosphere that the time of preparation has begun and is now released!

This is the season of refinement and where the difficulty begins. It is at this time the leader enters into preparation for the final out come. This will be a season of many challenges in the days ahead, as one is trained by the Holy Spirit Himself to stand and declare and decree your assignment. And you will begin to know that the carnal seductions sent by the principality of mammon will oppose the longevity of your assignment and challenge you to abandon Gods original plan. And you will begin to experience many adversarial manifestations trying to cause shipwreck along the way.

And at times you will feel like a contradiction and a reproach! This is truly a holy assignment and will need an understanding from much prayer and the ability to see through sovereign interventions, the many wonderful releases from God Himself, as you pursue after Him faithfully on the journey!

When a prophetic utterance comes, the believer needs to weigh it, ponder it, take inventory, and seek God as to what needs to be set in order to bring the full manifestation to pass. I have heard that the prophetic words should be a time of preparation entering a three to five year journey. So take inventory as to what God instructs you to do during this time. Faithfully examine the conditions before you, and seek the Lord diligently as to His plan of action to move you over the mountain of containment.

Let faith build as you use the prophetic words spoken over you as a tool to pray in your destiny. Use what God has spoken to you to open a door of deliverance promised in the prophesy. Decree His words!

1 Timothy 1:18
This charge I commit to you...according to the prophecies previously made concerning you, that by them you may wage the good warfare.

People must know how to exercise the power and authority that the individual carries to pray out their destiny as spoken by God-given prophecy. We must take the pure prophetic word to God and inquire of Him and decree its power to enhance the advancement. Can God bestow growth and prosperity on presumptuous and blind believers? Of course not, but He brings revelation to unveil our lack of understanding! Disobedience only brings presumption, self-ambition, and self-sufficiency, which is the nature of the un-regenerated man. All of these areas are being delta with and must be stripped away over the processing times. It is now that we have a revealed understanding of how we are preparing and confronting issues of the heart, or the mind will and emotions (the soul). We are continually on a learning curve in the things of God.

Let me give you a little test right here. I'm going to ask you five very basic questions. If you are not 100 percent on target in answering a resounding "yes" to any of these questions, you may need Basic Obedience 101.

Question One:
Is Jesus Christ really Lord of your life?

In order to answer that question, you have to understand what obedience is. Obedience is complying with or submitting to authority. In reality, if you're not rightly aligned with those elected co-leaders and partners of authority, why do you think God would allow you to be in authority? To be in obedience you must submit to someone's counsel somewhere. God has fore ordained holy alliances, we must just ask for them to be revealed to us and we will be directed to them by His spirit. By doing this we are yielding ourselves to wisdom and the submission to the authority of another one of wise counsel and understanding. We know that we are called by God alone, but we are in-grafted into covenant relationships along the way to build personal accountability. God will bring you a team elected by Him to co-partner and to serve His purpose in the earth. As you depend on hearing Gods voice He will lead you to the right wise counsel and mature alliances.

Can you honestly answer yes to the following question: Is Jesus Christ really Lord of your life? Lordship is giving Him total reign in all areas of your life. It is surrendering to Lordship!

If Jesus is really Lord of your life, you will surrender every part of your life to Him—all your talents, gifts, business ideas, accomplishments, vanities, ego, pride and ambition. Lay them all down at His feet! Isn't it nice to not have to carry all of that anymore? Now you can just operate by not owning anything, but becoming a bondservant and His steward over all that He has entrusted to you, as you work for the CEO of the universe! What a relief!

Question Two:
Are you in fellowship and in <u>covenant</u> relationships with other strong believers called as you are?

We are part of the third millennium and an emerging culture which we transitioned into in the year 2000. This has been a time of much change. We have left the *church age* as we entered into this third millennium, which many refer to as the third day, and we have now entered the *kingdom age*. The first thousand years after Christ was Israel, the second thousand years was the church, and now we entered the third thousand years in 2000 which is the kingdom.

There has been a larger shift of dissatisfaction from the old status quo in the mindset of the western "churches" and many are opting for more intimate/ relational types of gatherings. These gatherings are taking form in new emerging groups, such as house churches, as well as taking on many other forms of gathering. Some are in businesses cells, on campuses, meetings in coffee shops, boardrooms, government offices and chambers, hotels and many other areas of the marketplace. Do you attend meetings for fellowship with Christians who are compatible with your spiritual growth and are in a deeper walk with God in these days? These may be groups orchestrated by the Lord with a different wineskin as referenced by many. These may not be conventional types of "pulpits" but will be ordered by Gods design. This emerging culture is breaking out of the old wineskin and will be in the arts, the government, in the financial institutions and all forms of businesses in the marketplaces of the world.

God is changing the face of "church" as we have known it. Truth be know we are the "church*"* under the headship of Jesus Christ, it is *not in a building*, and we may not be in the same structure that we have known to be called "church" as in days past. It is not an institution but an organism.

The author of the book *The House That Changed the World,* Wolfgang Simson, wrote a fifteen point thesis on the change. Here I quote number nine and number eleven as follows:

Return from organized to organic forms of Christianity

The "Body of Christ" is a vivid description of an organic, not an organized, being. Church consists on its local level of a multitude of spiritual families, which are organically related to each other as a network, where the way the pieces are functioning together is an integral part of the message of the whole. What has become a maximum of organization with a minimum of organism has to be changed into a minimum of organization to allow a maximum of organism.

Too much organization has, like a straightjacket; often choked the organism for fear that something might go wrong. Fear is the opposite of faith, and not exactly a Christian virtue. Fear wants to control, faith can trust. Control, therefore, may be good, but trust is better. *The Body of Christ is entrusted by*

God into the hands of steward-minded people with a supernatural charismatic gift to believe God that He is still in control, even if they are not. A development of trust-related regional and national networks, not a new arrangement of political ecumenism is necessary for organic forms of Christianity to reemerge.

Stop bringing people to church, and start bringing the church to the people

The church is changing back from being a *Come*-structure to being again a *Go-*structure. As one result, the Church needs to stop trying to bring people "*into the church,*" and start *bringing the Church to the people*. The mission of the Church will never be accomplished just by adding to the existing structure; it will take nothing less than a mushrooming of the church through spontaneous multiplication of itself into areas of the population of the world, where Christ is not yet known. We have to ask God's direction in current times as to where these believers and covenant relationships are? Ask the Holy Spirit to direct you to the right spiritual group to be in association with. Through prayer you will be led to your spiritual "home" or an alignment with other like minded people so to speak; a group to be in intimate relationship or in covenant with. Through this there will be a delightful submission to one another for growing and maturing in the things of God? The Holy Spirit will direct you to the right people. The steps of a good man are ordered by the Lord.

When you have been led to people God has chosen for you to be in covenant with, their will be protection. Submit yourself to one another in love for maturing, so that you may blossom and grow and continue to walk in your Godly authority. Jesus has always been the head of the church, and we the ecclesia, His body. The Lord is developing a strong mature body or pure bride. You can receive covenant blessings poured down from the head through "His" direction, as we are a member's one to another.

Let's look at what the Bible says about fellowship.

Hebrews 10:25

Not forsaking the assembling of ourselves together as is the manner of some, but exhorting one another and so much more as you see the Day approaching.

Acts 2:42

And they continued steadfastly in the apostles' doctrine and fellowship, in the breaking of bread, and in prayers.

The definition of *Fellowship* is as follows:

- **Unity:** Close association and partnership, participation, communion, contribution, and brotherhood.
- **Koinonia:** Brought together by the Holy Spirit. Sharing in common and intimate bond of fellowship with the Christian society.

Connecting between the Lord Jesus and each
other.
- **Assembly**: A congregation, company, or multitude called together or assembled together to
convoke.
- **Exhortation**: To urge, advise, or caution
earnestly. To admonish urgently; to give urgent
advice or warnings.

Leaving the "Church" as we have known it

If you have been a member of a structured physical church congregation and you are directed else-
where by Gods leading this needs to be addressed.
As God has changed and transitioned us from the
"church age" in 2000, into the Kingdom age, there
has been a mass shifting of the body of Christ outside
of the four walls of a physical building or structured
environment, into the areas of business, finances,
entertainment and governments.

The subject of how we currently meet as a body
may be very different compared to the structure that
we have previously been accustomed with. God is
taking us from "religious" structures to "relationship" oriented meetings and groups. For far too
long we have served a different paradigm. Many are
returning to the original plan and style of the early
church. Different types of "community" are forming,
different types of participation, to celebrate; as well
as minister to Him, and serve His people with true
enjoyable relationships. People are also starting
apostolic centers, or places called mission bases,

where people come and go and are released from. A place to move people in and out of the structures to be released into their gifting and assignments, by participating in the sphere of influence that they are designed to impact. There is a mass shifting in how we will see the structure of the believers called the "church", God is moving on us in this time frame building a living organism of "lively stones." How God leads you to fellowship may be different in the current move of God.

Question Three:
Are you a faithful giver?

Do you give finances faithfully into the places you have received instruction by anointed leaders. Those leaders are your spiritual governors to educate, teach, and train you in the things of God. Be led by God to hear His voice on where you are to give. For many years now, we have had much financial extortion by leaders, who operate under averse and greed and mammon mind sets both in and outside of the "church" that we have known. Many ministers with a *"western mind set"* have used marketing schemes to entice people to build their own empires. Those days are over, it is time to be lead of God and hear what the spirit of the Lord is saying. There are many deserving ministries that are not "churches" who don't operate with a guaranteed ten percent income. God will lead you to pour resources into many who are walking in revealed present truth, those who may be the nameless, faceless ones who have lived by Gods provision without a marketing mindset.

God instructs us to give to the Fatherless, the widows, the orphans, the sojourners and the Levite. As we give to those in need we will see things in a different light. As we give to pure undefiled streams that are not operating under a spirit of mammon, we will see the changes that are necessary.

If you feel called to the financial arena and can be entrusted with the stewardship of wealth, we must not be presumptuous, but inquire to understand and obey the basics! As God allows us to be tested and stretched, always seek God about your giving! I have never been disappointed when I have given as led by God in obedience. It could be my last and best—my last cent but my best offering. If this is His requirement at a specific time He will do His part! However, you must trust Him implicitly. By being totally dependant on Him and His leading.

1 Timothy 5:17, 18
Let the elders who rule well be counted worthy of double honor especially these who labor in the word and doctrine.

For the scripture says, "You shall not muzzle an ox while it treads out the grain," and "The laborer is worthy of his wages."
1 Corinthians 9:7
Who ever goes to war at his own expense? Who plants a vineyard and does not eat of its fruit? Or who tends a flock and does not drink of the milk of the flock?

As the Lord begins to pour financial blessings forth, you must realize the great and awesome responsibility to be a good steward of that which He entrusts to you. You must pass many tests of integrity to be trusted with great wealth.

However, God will bring gifted people to help you govern the money. He will also bring administrative people to help you develop proper business practices.

Question Four:
Are you spending regular, quality time with God?

Is your time spent with God hit and miss? Or have you disciplined yourself to meet with God during an appointed time daily? Does your life reflect a life of prayer? Or do you cast about in life like a rudderless ship on an open sea?

Do you grab a little here and there from the prayers of others? Or do you try to depend on the success of others because they have learned to tap into God? Or have you learned to wait on God and hear His voice for yourself? Do you allow time to get quiet with God so He can speak to you?

Jeremiah 33:3
Call to Me and I will answer you and show you great and mighty things, fenced in and hidden, which you do not know (do not distinguish and recognize, have knowledge of and understand). (Amplified Bible)

In this scripture we find by calling out, we are attempting to get God's attention, so that we may receive important information. God promised Jeremiah that if he would call out to Him, He would reveal to him great and mighty things. The Hebrew word is "Batsar" which translated means isolated or inaccessible. We need this kind of revelational insight. We need to know how to pray effectively and to dig for the deep hidden and secret truths so necessary for this hour.

Psalm 91:15
He shall call upon Me and I will answer him; I will be with him in trouble; I will deliver him and honor him.

Although we have discussed some of this in a previous chapter in more detail, I felt it important to include it as a very important "key" for your success. I find that discipline is sometimes elusive in our daily routines. Often we have many time robbers and God robbers without the structure of making this our priority. I like to use the words supreme focus. We have to view our schedule circumspectively. We ask what does it mean to set an appointed time to spend with God? It means to make a fixed appointment to seek Him. Find a quiet place. Make the determination to do it and discipline yourself to show up every single day!

God wants to spend quality time with you, and He may use creative ways to do it. In the middle of the night or in the early morning hours He may arouse you. This may be the only time God can be sure of getting your undivided attention without interruption. If God should stir you in the night this way, be obedient and yield to it! By this yielding you are relinquishing, resigning, and giving up a sacrifice of your time to the superior authority, our precious Lord. There must be a reason why God chooses to wake you up at this hour. Don't you suppose God has some very important information to give you?

It is your responsibility to set this appointment with God daily. For example, you could never run a business without meeting fellow executives, board members, managers, agents or staff regularly. Without such meetings there would be no direction or progress in your business. You wouldn't have a successful roadmap. Your business would fail economically; you would fail miserably.

How much more important it is meeting daily with your Lord for instruction! Your relationship with the Lord is the most important one you posses and developing it will provide direction for your business.

In your daily appointment with the Lord, you're inviting and summoning Him to meet with you. You are welcoming Him to communicate with you by letting Him know you value and consider His advice of paramount importance.

Question Five:
Do you take time to rest from your labors?

Do you rest from your labors? Do you allow yourself to enjoy a time of restoration or recreation from the work you are called to do? God gives us wisdom to rest completely from our activities one day a week.

Genesis 2:2,3
And on the seventh day God ended His work which He had done, and He rested on the seventh day from all His work which He had done. Then God blessed the seventh day and sanctified it, because in it He rested from all His work which God had created and made.

In the beginning when God rested He abstained from further creating. He ended His work. The seventh day was designated for the good of man and as a special covenant celebration. This covenant is sanctified by those who observed this. God planned the seventh day to be a day of rest.

Exodus 20:8-10
Remember the Sabbath day, to keep it holy. Six days you shall labor and do all your work, but the seventh day is the Sabbath of the Lord your God. In it you shall do no work....

The Sabbath is to be a holy day set aside for God. One who is in covenant position with God is to stop his everyday activities. Honor God with rest every seventh day. God has a set pattern in creation. Six days He worked; on the seventh day He rested.

I hope this chapter has brought more accountability regarding your obedience to God. Make any needful adjustments or changes! Then get ready for greater successes accomplishments and financial breakthroughs!

It's time to gird up any weak areas. Obedience is truly better than sacrifice! But it takes sacrifice many times in our lives to be obedient.

The Word of God

Our words are powerful as we boldly declare the Word of God, activating in the natural and spiritual realm what God has ordained us to be. By applying the power of His logos word in all of our situations. We release Gods plans for humanity for all those whom we establish His logos power over in their circumstances. Decree His promises! For the whole earth is groaning for the redemption of the sons of man.

Obedience to God's basic laws will also help develop greater study skills. Those of you who have never received detailed instruction from God's Word will benefit greatly from a lifestyle of obedience. Learn to work the Word of God in a way that develops a hunger for the deep, secret, and hidden things of God!

Become more and more familiar with the assistance and guidance of the Holy Spirit to help you reach your goals and destination. Be confident that the Holy Spirit will give you direction. He will accompany you and direct your progress. The Holy Spirit will supply advice and counsel to you that is not available in people alone. He will release the supernatural, deliver the impossible, and perform the unbelievable.

Chapter 5

SANCTIFICATION AND HOLINESS IN THE MARKETPLACE

N ow that you have experienced an increase in your spiritual relationship with the Lord, and you're taking your spirituality into the marketplace, how do you maintain this level and go even deeper in God?

Before you go higher in God, realize there will be levels of testing along the way, which will displace and remove all forms of comfort! Fasten your spiritual seat belt, for it is going to be an exciting adventure.

In order to maintain your spiritual ascension in God, He will begin to expose or deal with the motives of your own heart daily to keep you pure and focused on righteousness. For example, He will show you how the power of your words—which may be both correct and incorrect—and how they can produce and control your circumstances. He will reveal how words can form our thoughts, and our thoughts can hinder our progress if they are not Gods thoughts. We must spend time meditating on His words and His thoughts.

Proverbs 18:21
"Death and life are in the power of the tongue, and they who indulge in it shall eat of the fruit of it (for death or life.)"
(Amplified Bible)

God is going to show you that you need His thoughts to become your thoughts by the renewing of your mind.

Jeremiah 29:11
"For I know the thoughts and plans that I have for you, says the Lord, thoughts and plans for welfare and peace and not for evil, to give you hope in your final outcome."

Proverbs 16:3
"Commit your works to the Lord and your thoughts will be established."

Psalm 139:23
"Search me O God and know my thoughts (heart); Try me and know my anxieties."

Philippians 4:6.
"Do not fret or have any anxiety about anything, but in every circumstance and in everything, by prayer and petition...with thanksgiving, continue to make your wants known to God." (Amplified Bible)

1 Peter 5:7
"Refuse worry and "[cast] the whole of your care [all your anxieties, all your worries, all your concerns, once and for all] on Him, for He cares for you affectionately and cares about you watchfully." (Amplified Bible)

Romans 12:1-2
"I appeal to you therefore, brethren, and beg of you in view of (all the mercies of God, to make a decisive dedication of your bodies (presenting all your members and faculties) as a living sacrifice, holy (devoted, consecrated) and well pleasing to God, which is your reasonable (rational, intelligent) service and spiritual worship. Do not be conformed to this world (this age, fashioned after and adapted to its external, superficial customs), but be transformed (changed) by the (entire) renewal of your mind (by its new ideals and its new attitude), so that you may prove (for yourselves) what is the good and acceptable and perfect will of God, even the thing which is good acceptable and perfect in His sight for you.)" (Amplified Bible)

I've heard it said that what you tolerate will eventually dominate you. Each new spiritual demand will require you to go higher in the things of God and deepen your level of maturity and dependence on His direction. Mediocrity is not an option! As you achieve higher levels of spirituality, God expects you to maintain that cutting edge. So let us look at a scientific equation to tie in all that our thoughts entail as well.

Quantum Physics and You – How the Science of the Unseen can Transform Your Life!

Whether or not you have much interest in quantum physics or quantum theory, understanding the principles of quantum physics can affect your life dramatically.Quantum physics are changing the way we view our lives-and I mean this quite literally!

One of the most exciting discoveries of quantum physics is the realization that our thoughts affect the world around us. In the quantum realm—far smaller than protons and neutrons—quantum scientists have conducted numerous experiments with the smallest-particles ever known.

In these quantum studies, it was discovered that the thoughts and expectations of the experimenters were actually causing the experiment's outcome! For instance, if the experimenter thought the particle would spin a certain way, it would! Scientists witnessed that a person's thoughts were actually causing the reaction of matter—at the quantum level...

The implications of this and other quantum studies has lead quantum scientists to understand that we have a direct effect on the world around us—our thoughts are affecting the physical world in which we live. In fact, they are discovering that the power of thought literally enables us to create reality—our own reality.

By revelation each day becomes a new *spiritual experience* for you, because you have literally begun to turn a corner in the realm of the spirit. As you are drawn deeper into God's plan of action, you will experience greater anticipation to understand the dynamics of a realm that is opening up to you through your persistent hunger. A hunger is developed by consistency. It does take discipline at first then it becomes spontaneous and a daily delight! Just remember God is continually rebuilding you spiritually for the greatest harvest of souls since the resurrection of Jesus Christ!

Amazingly, it is God who hand-picked you and poured God-given talents into your life to take into the marketplace and the financial arenas of the world. Now He is developing the character and qualities in you daily that will be necessary to be used by Him in every situation. You will no longer look at your circumstances as if you were just a mere man or woman. But you will now see things as a key diplomat or ambassador assigned by your Master to minister the gospel of the kingdom in these times to a very significant group of people. Are you ready?

God needs you to develop key qualities as a requirement to maintain sanctification and holiness in the marketplace. This is the only way you can be successful as God's representative.

The following seven key qualities are listed below to help you demonstrate a sanctified, holy lifestyle in the marketplace.

So we are learning, that as we process our thoughts into the atmosphere around us, that we can carry through our times of prayer and renew our thoughts, becoming agreeable with Gods thoughts.

FIRST KEY QUALITY FOR SUCCESS
Come to God humble, hungry, and desperate to hear His plan.

Scripture tell us that in order to go higher in God we must first go lower. In order to increase we must first decrease. This means we need to exercise humility before God can lift us up. When we are broken vessels of honor we are being prepared to serve in the stewardship that He has designed for us. Ultimately along the journey we will begin to understand that we simply need to disappear all together.

James 4:10
Humble yourselves in the sight of the Lord, and HE WILL LIFT YOU UP.

John 3:30
"He must increase but I must decrease"

SECOND KEY QUALITY FOR SUCCESS
Be willing to wait on God.

Waiting on God is not passive. It's not waiting around for God to do something. Actually, waiting on God means to actively seek His Presence and His plan. As you seek God's plan, take time to discern His perfect will for your life. Stay quiet and listening. God has so much to pour into us through prophetic revelations but the atmosphere to seek and receive from Him has to be quieted from human distractions.

Sometimes God is not in as much of a hurry as we are. As we endeavor to accomplish great works for God, realize some things may not yet be set in place. Timing is important with God, so be sure not to get out ahead of Him, because very often God will be working out details behind the scenes for us.

Psalm 37:34
Wait for and expect the Lord and keep and heed His way, and He will exalt you to inherit the land….(Amplified Bible)

THIRD KEY QUALITY FOR SUCCESS
Don't begin a work without confirmation from God.

Before you step out to begin a significant work for God, know that it is definitely God's direction and timing. Don't allow God's plan to be aborted because you've missed God's leading. If God's not in the work, you don't want to be. Enthusiasm can precede deception of we aren't willing to wait on God at times.

Isaiah 44:26
[The Lord] Who confirms the word of His servant and performs the counsel of His messengers....

FOURTH KEY QUALITY FOR SUCCESS
Be willing to let God take the credit for the work.

Remember pride is the number one sin God hates. You will never reach your highest potential in God if you do not give Him all the glory. After all, it's His work in the first place, and you couldn't accomplish it without Him. Therefore, never take the credit for the work God establishes. True humility will open all the doors for you. It is really all about Him!

2 Chronicles 32:26
But Hezekia humbled himself for the pride of his heart, both he and the inhabitants of Jerusalem, so that the wrath of the Lord came not upon them in the days of Hezekia.
(Amplified Bible)

FIFTH KEY QUALITY FOR SUCCESS
Be willing to relinquish ownership in favor of Lordship.

Understand that you are God's steward. Therefore, submit to stewardship rather than take ownership. As a steward it is your job to watch over the goods of another. Go to God to find out how He wants you to manage His goods.

Also, be faithful on the job as you make verbal commitments. This is part of being sanctified and holy in the marketplace. God has given you an anointing to receive and steward wealth, so you cannot afford to hinder that gift by compromising your integrity.

As time is coming to a close, faithfulness will be one of the hardest things for some people to maintain. No matter what the pressures, stay circumspect before your Lord.

Proverbs 20:6
Many a man proclaims his own loving-kindness and goodness but a faithful man who can find.

SIXTH QUALITY FOR SUCCESS
Allow the searchlight of the Holy Spirit to shine on your life.

Psalm 38:18
For I do confess my guilt and iniquity; I am filled with sorrow for my sin. (Amplified Bible)

Let the Holy Spirit bring displeasing areas of your life to the forefront. Maybe you have a weakness or habitual sin you haven't repented of. Well, now is the time to get on your knees and cry out to God for

His mercy. You cannot go one more day harboring hidden sin.

2 Corinthians 7:9, 10

Yet I am glad now, not because you were pained, but because you were pained into repentance [that turned you to God]; for you felt a grief such as God meant you to feel, so that in nothing you might suffer loss through us or harm for what we did.

For Godly grief and the pain God is permitted to direct, produce a repentance that leads and contributes to salvation and deliverance from evil, and it never brings regret; but worldly grief (the hopeless sorrow that is characteristic of the pagan world) is deadly [breeding and ending in death]. (Amplified Bible)

God is bringing His people into a time of greater accountability. In other words, God will judge gray areas of questionable conduct. The Christian community needs to intensely hate what offends or separates us from holiness.

Ninety-eight-percent holiness is not enough; it is time to expose the darkness in our lives. God is not going to allow His Church to continue in sin while He's preparing us for glory. The Bride of Christ cannot be tainted!

If you've never felt the conviction of the Holy Spirit regarding "gray areas" of questionable conduct in your life, I pray as you read this you will deeply repent. Do not waste any more time! The Holy Spirit is ever present to deliver you, to touch your life, and to separate you to a higher call.

Philippians 3:13, 14
Brethren, I do not count myself to have apprehended; but one thing I do, forgetting those things which are behind and reaching forward to those things which are ahead, I press toward the goal for the prize of the upward call of God in Christ Jesus.

SEVENTH KEY QUALITY FOR SUCCESS
Let the Holy Spirit be your barometer in all things.

Jesus said He would leave us a Comforter who would lead and guide us into all truth. He made the following statement to His disciples.

John 16:13
However, when He, the Spirit of truth, has come, He will guide you into all truth; for He will not speak on His own authority, but whatever He hears He will speak; and He will tell you things to come.

We need God's truth speaking to us all day long both on and off the job. If we plug into a higher spiritual level everyday, we will see how simple it is to stay tuned to the Holy Spirit's frequency.

God's power is always available, and He wants us to use it! God wants desperately to assist us in our every move. We won't miss God if we apply His plan rather than our man-made agenda.

Therefore, follow these seven key steps for success to activate God's power in your life! He will never fail you if you honestly try to walk holy before Him.

What Talents Do I Possess?

You may think you do not have significant talents to contribute to the business world. For example, you may think, "But all I can do is organize things or delegate duties." Well, that's a talent!

Administrative and entrepreneurial skills are God-given talents! God gives you the natural desire to use the talents He puts inside you. Besides, it is exciting when a person operates in his God-given talents. God gave you those skills for a reason. Before the foundation of the world, He planned a particular course ordained just for you. God designed those talents for you to use with expertise for His glory.

Consider what God says about you and your talents.

Jeremiah 1:5
Before I formed you in the womb I knew you;
Before you were born I sanctified you....

Perhaps you've been faithful to portray God in the marketplace, and now God is moving you on to a new level. For example, what if He's now calling you to the nations? Maybe you're saying, "But how can He call me to the nations? Who am I to go to the world?"

I thought that several years ago too. But from this vantage point, I can see clearly that God has expanded my vision to see part of His end-time plan for my life—it includes going to the nations. I know that nations are part of God's heart, and our talents can be used to affect multitudes world-wide for God.

But perhaps you are still questioning your election to this call asking, "How can I go to the nations? I don't have any world-wide contacts; my business is local and limited." Yes, you are limited, but your Heavenly Father is limitless.

The call to the nations should reside within the heart of every business person and impact every business opportunity. The function of every businessman or businesswoman of God in the end times is to sell out for God! For example, commit your earning capacity to winning souls. If you'll do this, God will make sure your resources are limitless.

Perhaps you've seen mission fields you've never noticed before. They may be mission fields on foreign soils, but you know God has placed them on your heart. First of all, those desires are God-given. God places those mission fields on your heart for a reason. As a business person, God will either make a way for you to go or enable you to support them financially.

Furthermore, God may highlight to you one specific ministry that is international in scope. Perhaps this ministry is just beginning; for example, the vision is just being birthed. God tugs on your heart to pour your resources and finances into that vision. He can even align your sights to see souls and nations you may never visit but that you can nonetheless transform for God's Kingdom.

For instance, maybe God has placed on your heart one ministry or one potentially key spiritual leader who is supposed to bring the gospel of the kingdom to foreign soil. Or perhaps that key person is yet unsaved, untrained, or not of noble position. However, with your support this potential spiritual leader could become a future teacher, minister, or prophet much like those in the Bible.

These key people may be God's choice to lead their generation to the King of kings and Lord of lords. It is God who raises leaders up, but it is you who must cooperate with God to get the work done. You may not be able to go to foreign fields physically, but your finances can! In fact, your finances can bring these visions from the heart of God and catapult them to the forefront.

As you obediently plant your seed in these fertile soils, do so with great joy and expectancy. Don't ever hold back! Release your financial support to these faithful servants. Act in a timely manner, obediently and faithfully fulfilling your commitments. If God definitely spoke to you about supporting a particular ministry, He will provide the means for you to liberally give to that ministry so you can complete your commitment.

Notice what the Word of God says about giving.

2 Corinthians 9:6-10

But this I say: He who sows sparingly will also reap sparingly, and he who sows bountifully will also reap bountifully.

So let each one give as he purposes in his heart, not grudgingly or of necessity; for God loves a cheerful giver.

And God is able to make all grace abound towards you, that you, always having all sufficiency in all things, may have an abundance for every good work. As it is written: "He has dispersed abroad, He has given to the poor; His righteousness remains forever." Now may He who supplies seed to the sower, and bread for food, supply and multiply the seed you have sown and increase the fruits of your righteousness.

The Bible says the return on your giving is to be viewed as a responsibility of great magnitude. God doesn't determine your return; you do! If you give with liberty out of obedience, and release what He instructs you to do, you'll be rewarded. If you reverently respect and fear the holiness of this financial assignment God will entrust you with the wisdom and discernment to be responsible for large sums of money. We must be thoroughly tried and tested to walk in this arena without any presumption taught in past seasons. In the Kingdom age we have overcome much to be released into the stewardship of Kingdom monies. He has been training servant leaders with the purity of heart to be Kingdom financiers.

Along with our financial giving, God asks us is to give Him everything we are. If He has our hearts, He'll have our finances! Giving both our hearts and our finances shows God we're really serious about following His plan. Get ready because as we do this, we'll take off for the ride of our lives!

God will surely pour out His blessings on all who commit to His faithful servants. Your personal fulfillment and satisfaction is greatly multiplied as you realize how important your giving is. Furthermore, the Bible says where your heart is, your treasure is. So by liberal giving, you're storing up treasure in heaven for yourself that will not perish but create a legacy for all of eternity.

Matthew 6:19-21
"Do not lay up for your selves treasures on earth where moth and rust destroy and where thieve break in and steal, but lay up for your selves treasures in heaven where neither moth nor rust destroy and where thieves do not break in and steal for where your treasure is there your heart will be also."

Chapter 6

PROTECTING THE GIFT

PROTECTING THE GIFTS AND ANOINTING BESTOWED ON YOU BY GOD

God has selected you for a unique purpose to be established in the earth, and you are the only one who can complete this particular assignment. Your uniqueness has equipped you for sustaining this assignment, and it is tied into intimacy and the loving relationship developed with you and God. His affirmation has endowed you with skills and tools to perform certain functions or tasks to be His effective leader in your God ordained "metron" or sphere of influence.

This preparation and these impartations are to come forth in God's divine timing. You must become a fine-tuned entity as you endeavor to hear everything God has to say to you accurately and concisely. For, you see, God's workmanship must be released through you at the appointed time. There is a set time of favor.

God's most profound revelations are given to you by the Holy Spirit as you spend quiet time alone in God's Presence. This is when God reveals His most intimate personal details to you. God's revelations are supernaturally imparted when you learn the value of tapping into His Presence where He can release and reveal His secrets and mysteries intended for your edification and spiritual maturity alone. In the last several decades and seasons in God there has been a universal shifting towards total dependence on this deep relationship. It is so vital in today's world that clamors for so much of our time. God has put a longing in the spirits of those who are yielded to be set apart in quiet anticipation to lean on and learn the many facets of Gods divine nature.

1 Corinthians 14:2
"For he who speaks in a tongue does not speak to men but to God, for no one understands him; however, _in the spirit he speaks mysteries_."

1Corinthians 2:7
"But we speak the wisdom of God in a mystery the _hidden wisdom which God ordained before the ages of our glory._"

Ephesians 1:9
**"*Having made known to us the mystery of*
His will according to His good pleasure
which He purpose in himself."**

Without a daily appointed time to come before
the Lord to hear His voice, you lose the supernatural gifting and discernment available for you to
advance spiritually for each specific day. By eagerly
approaching worship and ministering to Him as
your prerequisite, the preceding instructions will
be established in the hearing ear as you are intently
listening. You want to passionately receive divine
instructions/downloads revealed in these important
appointments.

Now is not the time to operate out of the ones
own self-sufficiency and presumptive mind sets.
When we stay close to Gods instructions we begin to
see how little we have truly connected to hearing His
daily directions. It will be impossible to complete
the tasks ahead without receiving revelations from
the Lord about personal destiny. There is always a
quickening in our spirits that we are on target as we
have more and more revealed prophetic information
poured into us.

The time you are willing to sacrificially commit
to the Lord will be rewarded with tremendous spiritual insight. These insights and empowerments allow
you to move in new impartations of spiritual strength.
God's mysteries must be sought after faithfully. There
is romance in loving and seeking God. You will never
be able to walk in certain spiritual dimensions until

you seriously seek God daily in your set appointed times with Him.

Although you may be challenged in your commitment to seek God daily, you can be assured that personal sacrifice will bring rewards and greater hunger. Besides, your human spirit is normally directed by ones flesh, you must choose to be dislodged from limitations or distractions! However, the stretching that your obedience brings, will eventually pay off in spontaneity. Don't fall back into neglecting your daily commitment to prayer because of slothfulness and laziness.

Keep and ponder God's pearls of wisdom as He gives you details of His plan for your life. Make note of them. Write them down! Learn to carry things in the spirit that He's given to you. In other words, continually pray over God's secrets; let them go deeply into your spirit.

However, don't be hasty to share all the details God gives you with everyone, be prudent and wise. When you are hasty to verbalize the great vision God is preparing to release to you, confrontations and onslaughts of oppression from enemy induced sources normally follow. Speaking about God's plan before the time can bring unnecessary demonic assignments or witchcraft and tremendous warfare that will try to delay or completely abort God's plan for your life.

This is the time to increase prayer for your vision. Pray now! God has entrusted you with something He wants to establish in the earth, but you need to pray it out first and hear from Him.

Once you hear something from God, and He gives you an impartation, you'll need to wisely protect it. *Protect the gift God gives you!* Find out who are the few wise people in your inner circle, intimate people to whom you can release your godly secrets if God says to. Usually they will be found from among those who are standing in agreement with you in prayer, or have a sovereign connection to your assignment.

Sometimes you won't be able to share much information with others because God has so much more He wants to impart to you before the vision can be completely released. God can't afford for you to release His secrets prematurely. Sometimes His vision to you must be established in detail, and that will require you to earnestly seek His face so the vision can be fulfilled at the appointed time. When Mary was visited by angelic heraldry with the revelations from God acknowledging that she would be the "virgin" Mother of Messiah; and when the shepherds were supernaturally given information to find the newly born Savior…"Mary kept and pondered these things in her heart." The word "*ponder*" means to consider something deeply and thoroughly; to meditate, to weigh carefully in the mind and to consider thoughtfully. We must learn to carry these things in our hearts until the appointed time of release, to protect that which you have been given by God, because your assignment is a holy one and needs releases at appointed times.

Furthermore, don't assume everyone who calls himself a "Christian" has pure motives. Just because you walk in integrity and spiritual maturity, many times others don't. Even people calling themselves "Christians" may have personal, hidden agendas that will hinder your God given vision. Not every Christian will be in right alignment or assigned to help your business, ministry, or gifting.You need to know how to test peoples' motives to determine if they are pure. This is why walking in the gifts of the spirit will be very important. Word of wisdom and words of knowledge, discerning of spirits, gift of faith, working of miracles will all be your power package to operate in. Every believer must seek this pattern as a foundational support in all levels of becoming a strong and overcoming believer.

Many people have not been fine-tuned spiritually because not every Christian's walk with God may be as deep or consistent as yours. You are a model to others who may not be there yet. Therefore, it's very important that you are covered and protected by strong, anointed leaders in alignment with you. It's vital that you cover and protect the gifting and impartations given to you by God! These are to be sovereignly sent to you by God.

Be aware of self-righteous, prideful, or religious people. By "religious" I mean people who follow empty rituals but *don't really know God* in the way He has called you. We must know each other after the spirit of God. Purity of heart is not uneasy to detect. Those who are possessing negative qualities indicate great areas of unsanctification. These attitudes must be brought into subjection, or they will try to undermine God's work in your life. You don't need any anarchy from negative qualities in your camp just when your project is being launched.

Ask the Holy Spirit to bring you people of spiritual substance who are sent by God and are loyal and dedicated to your vision. Pray them in! Ask for discernment and discerning of spirits. Test motive of the heart.

Now is not the time for compromise! Rather, it is the time for renewed dedication, because the warfare against us can be very intense at times as God is refining and destroying our fleshly desires. These times of training will try to weaken your resolve and hinder your projects, and can be tested by the wrong people being planted in your midst. Know those who labor among you. Test every spirit and receive instructions from God if there are any checks in your spirit. These pauses are there for you to seek God for understanding and wisdom before you move ahead.

That's why you must pray diligently for unity and compatible giftings to be in association with people who will be a complement and blessing to the vision you have been assigned to by God. There's power in numbers with the people who will stand and assist you in the unity necessary to help fulfill their part of your God-given vision.

For example, I experienced something once that helped prepare me to train others. Actually, this experience came about as a result of my own natural outgoing personality. I made the mistake of presuming people thought like I did—assuming they would treat my ideas with the same respect I treated theirs. How wrong I was!

Some people are attracted to the anointing and want to pull on your gift, pervert it, abort it, and prostitute it. But God didn't give your gift to them! They didn't pay the price for it that you did. And for them to operate in a gifting falsely, the Bible calls lawlessness and witchcraft. We have all experienced things on the journey that didn't set right. Witchcraft can come against you. But witchcraft can be more than what we normally think. Witchcraft can be someone else imposing their will against you in an effort to control you. The imposing nature of self-willed and lawless people can be assigned to adversely affect your health, finances, relationships, and ministry. However, once again, these opportunities come to train us to discern between good and evil motives of mans heart. God is looking for purity of heart in vessels of honor, which will blend their gifts for the common good of the whole. This is why you need to protect the gift God's given you!

Stay girded up spiritually! Ask the Holy Spirit to always confirm your spiritual alignments—your relationships—in the mouth of two or three witnesses. Intimacy with God brings forth sensitivity and discernment in the spirit!

2 Corinthians 13:1
"This is the third time that I am coming to You. By the testimony of two or three witnesses must any charged and every accusing statement be sustained and confirmed."

Hear from God! Don't trust your own good nature—get a release from God before you share God's plans for your life.

We live in perilous times at best. Everything that can be shaken is shaking for the redemptive work of the cross! There are evil assignments sent to draw us closer to the things of God. Evil deceptions lurk in Christian communities as well to prey on weak believers—those who don't have a revelation of God's Word and His great discernment. With wisdom and understanding we will be able to always overcome, because as we overcome we can rule, our experiences will allow us to ascend and rule over all circumstance which oppose us from the second heaven where evil forces rule.

WEAPONS: THE SUPERNATURAL EQUIPMENT

One way we grow spiritually is by learning to discern between good and evil motives in people. Such growth can sometimes be painful because as we grow spiritually, we undergo godly stretching, molding, and refining by the Holy Spirit. When we walk in purity of heart we stir up conflict in unrighteous people.

But such growth will ultimately make you stronger and sharper in the spirit. You will be mighty in God when you pull down strongholds by practicing scriptural thinking.

Notice what the Bible says about the relationship between spiritual warfare and disciplined scriptural thinking:

2 Corinthians 10:3-5
For though we walk in the flesh, we do not war according to the flesh. For the weapons of our warfare are not carnal but mighty in God for pulling down strongholds, casting down arguments and every high thing that exalts itself against the knowledge of God, bringing every thought into captivity to the obedience of Christ.

Spiritual people must deal ruthlessly with carnal thoughts in their own minds. Therefore, as you grow spiritually you must recognize the spiritual war that can take place in your mind. You must be prepared to take every thought captive that may be hostile to God. One way to do this is to memorize Gods word and know specific scriptures needed with military discipline, with consistency. The power to disseminate and decree the word of God based on knowing the power of His preceding word breaks apart opposing forces.

Meditating on God's Word helps you fight against carnality. For example, practice slowly articulating and meditating on the words: *"the weapons of our warfare are not carnal"* 2 Corinthians 10:4 We don't operate from carnal knowledge but from our spirits and the spirit realm!

Let's take a closer look at some of the key words in this passage of scripture. It will help us understand what God is really telling us about our thought life.

- **Carnal:** not spiritual; temporal, worldly; pertaining to or characterized by the passions or appetites of the flesh.
- **To pull down:** to draw downward, to demolish, to wreck, to lower, or reduce. It also means to draw or tug on something by force. To cast down imaginations is to lower or to reduce them; to bring them down in size.
- **Strongholds:** a well-fortified place; fortress. A stronghold can be forming mental concepts of what is not actually present to the senses.
- **Exalt:** to rise in rank, honor, power, or quality; to elevate; to intensify and elevate something against the knowledge of Christ and His ways.
- **Knowledge:** the body of truth about Christ's ways.

You cannot continue to simply use natural means to fight carnal thinking. Rather, you must advance God's plan by using disciplined scriptural thinking to resist the onslaughts of the evil thoughts and walk above the second heaven warfare.

Psalm 94: 11
"The Lord knows the thoughts of man, that they are vain (empty and futile-only a breath)." (Amplified Bible)

Psalm 139: 23-24
"Search me (thoroughly), O God, and know my thoughts! And see if there is any wicked or hurtful way in me, and lead me in the way everlasting." (Amplified Bible)

God is more than enough to extend His mighty hand of protection. He said in His word that we are sealed unto His coming. It is His heart to remove anything containing and concealing you from the evil deceptions. After all you are fortified with the mind of Christ. If you walk in His ways nothing can separate you from His original plan. That is what the Lord Jesus Christ wants to pour into your life.

It is critical that God wants to reveal to you business promotions and financial assignments to carry out your position of stewardship. The training is continual to exercise authority over thoughts that are not of God.

As you approach your financial assignment with spiritual discernment—whether it be a business or any enterprise for God—declare and decree scriptures given to you personally as you receive them from God's Word! Then you will begin to see how to use this spiritual power effectively in each situation of resistance. One does not approach circumstances in fleshly carnality alone. One can be targeted through lack of spiritual discernment. Stay spiritually sharp and discerning!

As you fulfill your daily prayer commitment with God, you will be able to move with greater dexterity in every arena, including your financial and business assignments. God is taking over-comers to new levels through the ascension experiences, visitations and much activity from heaven. As hunger and purity increases we move through earthly barriers. This place of perfection that is being processed in us removes all barriers and onslaughts of our souls to press past warfare from the second heaven into the holy of holies. Because a new level with God is being sought and deposited, you will begin to grasp with ease the hunger that the Lord intended for you to flow in the depths of His sovereignty.

That is why you need to obey the voice of the Holy Spirit! When you have a check in your spirit, do not pursue anything until you consult the Lord first to get His revelation on the subject.

Here are the two verses of scripture that God gave me when I asked Him about a person who tried to manipulate information about the gifting and assignment the Lord entrusted me with to her advantage. I asked the Lord, "Is there spiritual witchcraft coming against me from this woman?" Without giving enough forethought to this matter, I innocently released a concept from this book prematurely. Immediately I began to experience 28 day of illness. It was also apparent that I was unusually ill for a prolonged period, which is not the norm for me. I sensed that I was experiencing a form of spiritual warfare as this person pursued me. She was inquiring about specific detailed information which seemed inappropriate. I felt that her interest was not to endorse that which was given to me by the Lord in a correct manner but to extract information to be used for self benefit and her personal advancement.

I dropped the relationship as quickly as possible and allowed no further contact with her. Regretfully, in my ignorance I didn't understand that her motives were wrong. She had an agenda, because she was looking for self-promotion. She desired to use this concept to position herself before other prominent leaders. Purity of heart is an important issue with those discriminating people God aligns you with. That is why it is vital to maintain a daily relationship with God so you can discern right and wrong motives in others.

Jeremiah 29:8,9
For thus says the Lord of host, the God of Israel: Let not your [false] prophets and your diviners who are in your midst deceive you; pay no attention and attach no significance to your dreams which you dream or to theirs. For they prophesy falsely to you in My name. I have not sent them, says the Lord. (Amplified Bible)

Jeremiah 27:9,10
Do not listen to your [false] prophets, your diviners, your dreamers, [and your dreams, whether your own or others'], your soothsayers, your sorcerers....For they prophesy a lie to you to be removed far from your land; and I will drive you out, and you will perish. (Amplified Bible)

God has placed business ideas and abilities into your hands for safekeeping and fulfillment. Protect them so He can fulfill His release with the stewardship of Kingdom finances to you.

The following scripture from God's Word explains God's perspective of the vision He's entrusted you to fulfill.

God wants you to seek hard after Him because He wants you informed, protected, guarded, and discerning. He's training and releasing you for greatness.

Jeremiah 29:11-14
For I know the thoughts I think toward you, says the Lord. Thoughts of peace and not of evil, to give you a future and a hope. Then you will call upon me and go and pray to Me and I will listen to you. And you shall seek Me and find Me when you search for Me with all your heart. I will be found by you, says the Lord, and I will bring you back from you captivity.

A closer look at the study reference section of your Bible reveals repeated references to God's people seeking after Him. Seeking God diligently implies a quest for God that includes a deeper level of intensity beyond what might be called ordinary prayer.

The word "search" combined with the phrase "with all your heart" suggests an earnestness that borders on desperation. In Hebrew the verb "to search" suggests *to* follow after or to closely pursue a desired objective. It implies diligently searching and seeking God.

Enclosed is a prayer strategy I created entitled "Hidden from the attacks of the Enemy." As you read over the following prayer confessions, I encourage you to make this part of your daily prayer practice.

HIDDEN FROM THE ATTACKS OF THE ENEMY
In the Secret Place of Your Presence

Dear Heavenly Father, I thank You that according to Your Word I have a secret place of protection from the enemy.

__Psalm 31:20__ declares that You shall hide me in the secret place of Your Presence far above the plots of man. You shall keep me secretly in a pavilion from the strife of tongues.

Therefore, Father, according to Your Word, I decree that You hide and protect _____by the power of Jesus' blood. You prevent _____ from being taken in a hidden snare (Psalm. 91:3) You prevent any weapon formed against _____ to prosper, including witchcraft, demonic assignments, and spoken curses. They shall be of no consequence!

You hide _____ in the protection of Your secret place and rescue _____ from any oppressive or demonic onslaught (Isaiah 43:1-2). You redeem _____ from family generational curses. You deliver _____ from all things pertaining to public accusations, curses, and slander (Isaiah. 54:17). You safeguard _____ by Your blood covenant (Revelations. 12:11) and the activity of heaven assigned to me.

I thank You that _____ is kept sealed and protected because You are _____ 's refuge and fortress. You constantly help _____ fulfill Your original purposes for _____'s life (Philippians. 1:6; Psalms. 138:8; Isaiah. 41:10,

13,14).You protect _____'s family and dwelling place. You give _____ a peaceable habi-tation, a secure dwelling, and quiet resting places (Isaiah. 32:18).

You protect _____ against evil plots, secret plans, and any detrimental schemes. _____ feels Your security and protection and is hidden in a pavilion, a habitation, a tower, an impenetrable place of safety.

No strife, violent, bitter conflict, enmity, nor clash can come against _____. All tongues, power of speech, or character of speech, spoken detrimentally shall be put to naught by _____.

Father, no ungodly words or beliefs can take root or prosper in _____ life (Matthew. 15:13). I speak the cancellation of every assignment by decreeing protection by the blood of Jesus and all the activity released from heaven over _____. By the power of the Name of Jesus Christ, I reverse every curse in transit against _____ (Mathew. 18:18, 19; Collations. 2:15; Philippians. 2:9, 10).

By the authority in God's Word, _____ has the authority to trample on serpents and scorpions and over all the power of the enemy, and nothing shall in any wise hurt _____.

Lord, Your Word says that we can be strengthened with all hope in You. Your Word also says to be of good courage, and You shall strengthen our hearts because we hope in You (Psalm 31:24).

Father, I thank You that _____ is strengthened with mighty power through Your Spirit in the inner man (Ephesians 3:16). I declare that _____ is empowered to grow stronger. I decree that _____ ___'s spiritual empowerment is a God-given right, which is a quality or state of being strong physically, mentally, emotionally, and spiritually. _____ has power and vigor all the days of _____ life.

Father, I affirm that _____ is endowed with an effective intellectual force. _____ walks in power and resistance to temptation daily. _____ 's God-given strength is _____ source of power, encouragement, and sustenance.

I surround _____ with faith, love, and courage—the quality of mind and spirit that enables _____ to face difficult circumstances without fear. _____ operates in bravery.

Father, I pray that _____ stands strong in hope and expectation, knowing that _____ can trust in the Lord whose ear is always open to the cry of the righteous (Psalm 94:9). _____ looks forward with desire and confidence to each and every day. I thank You that _____'s path grows ever brighter day by day (Proverbs 4:18).

I thank You that _____ walks in God-given freedom and authority (John 8:36). _____ can accomplish on the earth all that You have assigned _____ to do because _____ walks in total joy, liberty, and freedom from all assignments against _____ 's health and well being. _____ is restored, established, and settled in the Lord, decreeing Your miracle healing power in every area of containment over _____'s life.

Pray the Word of God like this every day to strengthen your relationship with Him using His Word, and to strengthen the person you're praying for.

Chapter 7

FOUR POWER-PACKED PRAYER PRINCIPLES FOR VICTORY

There are four profound questions that I ask every businessperson seeking to increase in Godly prosperity. These questions are designed to bring the revelation of God's protection, by empowering and strengthening your prayer covering and alliances so that you may add a greater momentum to your vision.

Each question represents a godly principle that when followed brings more effective changes for victory in business.

The Four Powerful Prayer Principles for Victory

- Establish Assigned Personal Intercessors
- Implement a Daily Corporate Prayer Plan

- Create a Detailed Written Weekly Prayer Strategy
- Develop a Prayer Plan Equal to a Business Plan

1. Prayer Principle One
Establish Assigned Personal Intercessors

To determine those who *truly have an election;* are sanctified, purified and qualified to walk in the spiritual humility to be entrusted as stewards of God's plans for end time wealth transfer, I always begin by asking business people this first basic question: Who are the personal intercessors assigned to you by God?

You see, intercessory prayer is vital to your business' success and continued survival. It is the foundation and infrastructure of all financial success. Furthermore, if you're going to forge ahead and reach and steward great levels of Godly prosperity, then you're going to need powerful prayer alliances to assist you at all times by the adding of various levels of help. Inquire of God and keep trusted people close to you who will faithfully help you pray out God's business plans.

2. Prayer Principle Two
Implement a Daily Corporate Prayer Plan

The following is the next thought-provoking question I routinely ask businesspeople: Do you pray daily with your staff? This question provokes businesspeople to think about the power of corporate prayer.

The second powerful prayer principle is to implement a daily corporate prayer plan. This principle should be viewed as the strength that protects every aspect of one's business. Establishing a designated time for corporate prayer unifies your business staff and allows the Holy Spirit to bind each person together in strength of purpose. The power released in unified corporate prayer will become evident.

In the beginning you may need to establish a short teaching outlining the importance of corporate prayer. However, realize as you initiate daily corporate prayer, you will see different levels of spiritual development emerge among your staff. Perhaps some may be unfamiliar with the power and application of corporate prayer, you may be able to implement training for these people you can exercise your leadership skills to establish a sound teaching on prayer.

You may even decide to schedule corporate prayer training by utilizing a seminar format. If you decide to teach corporate prayer in seminars, trust God to raise the level of spiritual hunger and desire of your group. You can hold corporate prayer training seminars just as you hold staff training meetings.

Expect God to provide a workable prayer format for you, and remember He just asks you to step out in faith and trust His ability to make the transformation in people. He's placed you in a position of leadership because He has great confidence in you. And He will continue to support you as you turn to Him in total dependence to establish His will with the help of the Holy Spirit.

The next thing to decide is who should come to the corporate prayer meeting. I suggest that all leaders and as many of the staff as possible be in attendance for corporate prayer. If your staff esteems the commitment to corporate prayer, then the Holy Spirit will begin to quicken their hearts and minds. Corporate prayer will bring your staff to new levels of spiritual understanding.

Implementing corporate prayer will draw those who are weaker in their spiritual development to a higher level of spiritual and professional commitment. By establishing this daily time before the Lord, you will provide a pivotal opportunity to bring unified success to your business. Then the Holy Spirit will begin to move freely among the people. Corporate prayer thrusts people into higher levels of spiritual growth.

The last thing to consider about implementing corporate prayer in your business is time. How much time should you allow for daily corporate prayer? I suggest devoting at least a half hour but preferably one hour if possible each day before the Lord.

As you do this you will be amazed how much more productively your business runs. When you submit the first fruits of your time to the Lord, you will find that God multiplies more time back to you. As you yield yourselves to this dynamic prayer commitment, you will actually run a more efficient business because the Lord multiplies time back to you.

Let me interject the meaning of four basic words to help you better understand corporate prayer as it relates to business.

- **Corporate:** Pertaining to a united group of persons; people united or combined into one opinion, spirit, and mindset.
- **Agreement:** The establishing or coming together in mutual agreement. A state of being in-one-accord. An arrangement accepted by all parties.
- **Communion:** The interchanging or sharing of thoughts or emotions in intimate communication.
- **Communication:** The imparting or interchanging of thoughts, opinions, and information through speech or writing.

As you come together in corporate prayer day after day, you add strength to strength. By implementing corporate prayer, you establish a combined corporate agreement, communion, and communication between you and your staff. You are actually submitting this agreement and placing it under the authority of the Spiritual Chief Executive Officers' divine counsel: the Father, Son, and the Holy Spirit.

The power of agreement among your employees will begin to accomplish a unifying force that will get the job done like never before. In your business setting, God will honor your commitment to trust in Him for your portion of stewarding His kingdom resources. As you step out into new levels of faith to establish corporate prayer, your prayer momentum promotes a mantle of prosperity on all levels and a wealthy platform in your workplace.

In this kind of spiritual environment, you will begin to see and feel the harmony of opinions and feelings homogenized among the workplace community. The Holy Spirit will honor this unity by promoting more efficiency, which enables tasks, assignments, projects and duties the tangible ebb and flow to get finished or processed more expediently.

In a powerful way through corporate prayer, you will begin to discern any areas that may need to be hedged or circumvented by the onslaughts of the challenges that try to hinder both business and staff. Your business will begin to make great gains in godly prosperity by adding this dimension

3. Prayer Principle Three
Create a Detailed Written Weekly Prayer Plan

The following is the third provocative question I ask businesspeople: Do you have a weekly prayer strategy?

I have developed a written format detailing weekly prayer needs. Habbakuk 2:2 says to: "write the vision and make it plain'. Therefore, you must develop a detailed written prayer plan. This information can be used by your staff in the corporate prayer setting. And it is a document with line items, to be emailed out the business needs to your assigned intercessors each week.

This weekly prayer strategy is a significant tool to rouse intercessors to pray specifically for your business needs. This weekly prayer strategy may be tailored to execute current needs for your business. You may want to use different categories than those included in the enclosed copy, but here are various examples to be considered.

It's important to create a detailed written weekly prayer plan because your business needs are in a constant state of change. Therefore, it's necessary to create a prayer plan that can be adapted to the needs of your business on a weekly basis.

<u>WEEKLY PRAYER PLAN FORM</u>

Business name:

Date:

Send to:

Below are detailed prayer-requests or timeline items/ needs for the week of _____.

Please bring these requests before the Lord to establish a prayer covering. We believe for a precise undertaking, breakthrough, intervention, or time line completion on these important matters/ projects. Thank you for your prayer covering and scriptural agreement with us.

ENTER THE APPROPRIATE INFORMATION IN THE SPACE PROVIDED BELOW.

- <u>Meetings of importance</u>
- <u>Financial needs or goals for this week</u>

- <u>Needs related to leadership</u>
- <u>Needs related to employees or staff</u>
- <u>New projects</u>
- <u>Travel</u>
- <u>Seminars, conventions, or group events</u>
- <u>Wisdom/understanding and Godly counsel</u>
- <u>Projects on the table of imminent importance</u>
- <u>Miscellaneous</u>

LIST THE ITEMS TO BE COVERED IN PRAYER BELOW AS NEEDED.

- Products to be produced
- Production to be implemented
- Personnel to be added or trained
- New areas of business expansion
- New equipment and supplies to be added
- Important scheduled meetings or presentations
- New direction or goals for the company

And the list could go on. God will instruct you in the appropriate application of categories for the needs of your vision.

With the addition of a weekly assigned prayer strategy, you have a "document of declaration and decree" to use to implement your corporate authority of strength and agreement over any difficult or opposing forces or strongholds. This prayer strategy is a powerful impacting tool to provide the spiritual impetus to get the job done.

A weekly prayer strategy will help build strength and momentum through the power of words and decrees that pull into your today that which needs to be accomplished. It is also your prayer of petition and proclamation for divine intervention at your workplace. God gives us the word of wisdom, discernment, discerning of spirits, words of knowledge, the gift of faith and working of miracles that we need to get the job done!

The following scriptures are powerful promises that will add strength to your weekly prayer plan. Review the scriptures below to receive additional insight into the power of prayer. Use them with the authority and implementation as rules of engagement to pray out your weekly prayer plan.

Matthew 18:19
Again I say to you that if two of you agree on earth concerning anything that they ask, it will be done for them by My Father in Heaven.

Acts 2:1
When the Day of Pentecost had fully come, they were all with one accord in one place.

1 John 3:22
And whatever we ask we receive from Him, because we keep His commandments and do those things that are pleasing in His sight.

Matthew 7:7, 8
"Ask, and it will be given to you; seek, and you will find; knock, and it will be opened to

*you. "For everyone who ask receives, and
he who seeks finds, and to him who knocks
it will be opened."*

Philippians 4:6, 7
*Be anxious for nothing, but in everything by
prayer and supplication, with thanksgiving,
let your requests be made known to God;
and the peace of God, which surpasses all
understanding, will guard your hearts and
minds through Christ Jesus.*

PRAYER PRINCIPLE FOUR
**Develop a Prayer Strategy (Plan) Equal to
Business Plan**

The final question I inquire of businesspeople to
induce strength is probably the one that spurs a new
method of thinking more than any other question I
ask: *Do you have a prayer plan equal to your business
plan?* In other words do you have a business
prayer strategy? If you don't, it is vital to develop a
business prayer strategy.

What Is a Business Pray Strategy?

A business prayer strategy is a specific, tailor-made
plan inspired by the Holy Spirit that allows
you to accomplish that which God ordained for you
in business. *It is* a written formula *designed to meet
the needs of your business* by applying the written
Word of God in a detailed written format. Take these

words and speak them audibility for a victorious final outcome to maximize your fulfillment of purpose.

A successful business prayer strategy provides the following:

- A mighty spiritual tool
- An enabling to speak out and decree the mysteries of God with authority
- A setting in motion in the spirit realm of the plans and purposes of God
- A bringing of tangible spiritual substance to that which God has given
- A strategy backed by scripture and the legal rights and authority
- A Logos Word from God that becomes a Rhema word
- A spoken proclamation to decree a thing and it will come to pass

Our words have strength. *Therefore*, we need to confirm God's plan, decreeing His Word with our voice. Our prayer should also remind God what He said, putting Him in remembrance of His Word.

Isaiah 43:26
Put Me in remembrance; let us contend together; state your case, that you may be acquitted.

We are contending together with God against the opposition. We can use God's Word to earnestly assert our spiritual position through a detailed declaration of prayer. Our words are powerful tools we use to declare and announce ostentatiously, boldly, and powerfully God's promises which He has given to us.

And when we speak God's Word over our business plans, we forge ahead by putting spiritual impetus to our dreams and visions. This is to effectively war in the heavenlies for new spheres of power and jurisdiction so that the kingdom of God is prompted and established in new realms regions and terrestrial domain to stand as the person of authority on the offensive at all times. His Kingdom come His will be done on earth as it is in heaven!

Chapter 8

INTERCESSION, INTERCESSORS AND CORPORATE PRAYER

What is intercession? Why is intercession important? Why should I implement intercessory prayer in the corporate setting? Why do I need personal intercessors assigned to me and to my business or vision? All these questions will be answered in this chapter. I continually see that there is a lack of intercession assigned to Christian business leadership and ministries as well. We simply must have intercessors assigned to those called to strong positions of authority. It is no longer optional to lack understanding of what importance prayer and intercession will do to change your circumstances. With these applied principles we will strengthen the protection necessary to forge ahead with great victory.

What Is Intercession?

Intercession is prayer at the highest level. It is a ministry that is available to everyone on the face of the earth. What happens to us when we become obedient to follow a daily, structured prayer life is absolutely wonderful in God. It is simply love on its knees!

We become acquainted with our God and learn valuable information that can only be imparted to us as we take a daily journey in obedient, faithful, and exciting prayer. We begin to receive information and revelation so necessary to perform the activities orchestrated by God for us to fulfill our every endeavor.

Intercessory prayer establishes the foundation of our relationship with God. It builds continual supernatural communication with Him. When we choose to come to God requesting information for all the details of our lives, we begin to see how important we are to Him. And we also see how important it is to receive the right information. We will begin to take on a new understanding about personal fellowship and communion with our Master and Maker.

Intercessory prayer releases us from so many fears and bondage's that take place in our lives as a result of being spiritually undisciplined and lacking intimate communication with our Heavenly Father. When we're not trained to come apart and be separated unto God—to get quiet before God—lack and futility will often be the results. We desperately need this time with God. He has been asking us to come to Him and lay aside the distractions that rob us of this time.

In the past two decades, we as a people, have such accelerated, fast-tracked lives with microwave mentalities and attitudes. We've been forced into perpetual motion, keeping a constant pace of action. It has become very foreign for us to even take a day to rest and refrain from the demands of a busy society. This is the seduction of a prosperous and western mind set.

We have suffered from this, and our personal relationships have also suffered as well. Our families are deprived of precious time that is not redeemable, children sometimes feel a greater brunt from this, and our health is also challenged because of pushing ourselves to the max and filling our personal lives with stress. We don't sleep, and we search for "quick fixes" or shortcuts and alternatives to reduce the insane dilemma that has taken our peace. It is really not Gods best! He called us to communion with Him and we have really gotten off the track He has always ordained for us to have. It was in the very beginning that Adam walked with God in fellowship in the cool of the day. We have toiled ever since not recognizing that the place of all success is in this relationship. And man is now trying to reconcile what has been perverted! It has been a battle for our time ever since.

But look what the Word says about putting other things first before God.

Hebrews 3:18
And to whom did He swear that they would not enter His rest, but to those who did not obey?

Hebrew 4:1
Therefore, since a promise remains of entering His rest, let us fear lest any of you seem to have come short of it..

Hebrews 4:5, 6
And again in this place: "They shall not enter My rest."
Since therefore it remains that some must enter it, and those to whom it was first preached did not enter because of disobedience.

Hebrews 4:11
Let us therefore be diligent to enter that rest, lest anyone fall according to the same example of disobedience.

In the past, believers have failed to enter the rest that God has promised. Resting presents the experience of fully surrendering to the Lordship of Jesus Christ, totally controlled by the Holy Spirit and His leading. But sometimes it requires a spiritual laboring of faith to enter God's rest.

However, in order to separate ourselves to build a solid prayer life, we won't be able to get the job done without knowing God's rest. Resting in God requires trust—trust that relinquishes ownership to Lordship. By entering God's rest we can release self-sufficiency to His sufficiency. It has to be understood that the shifts have been enormous and we as a people have had to move with the changes all around us in these seasons.

Dwelling in God's rest makes our prayer life more spontaneous and yielded. When we trust God with the ability to enter our prayer times, we are actually making a commitment to stay in His rest. Then we can understand why it is "labor to enter rest" because it takes *faith* to enter rest and trusting God. It is in God's place of rest that we are completely unwound from our own concepts and previous containment which often delay our coming to God.

As we become people of prayer and intercession, we are compelled by God to come into the deeper, more important things of the Spirit. Prayer and intercession help us in our corporate prayer assignments as well. Our prayer time and prayer life is more valued as our entire purpose is to yield to God first.

Separation unto God is also separation from the carnal mentality of personal goals and fleshly needs or desires. These pale in comparison to God beckoning or drawing us away into prayer and intercession with Him.

As an intercessor, a person becomes compelled to pray for the needs of others. An intercessor is the catalyst to expedite the plan, purpose, and will of God. An intercessor's prayers work by bombarding the power of heaven to circumvent the pounding of hell against a believer's life, work, anointing, or vision. When we enter into an ascension experience through relentless hunger for more of Him, we pass barriers of constraint that keep us bound to earth. We begin to leave the limited realm of this earth and come into alignment with the eternal purposes of God. By pressing into the realms of the spirit we enter into the place of His glory. This is where flesh and spirit separate and we walk in the realm of His manifested glory.

An intercessor is righteously obsessed with prayer and is determined in focus. An intercessor is passionate in the execution of prayer and in the releasing of grace and mercy so necessary to establish God's Kingdom on earth.

Look what the Bible says about Jesus our High Priest, the perfect Intercessor.

Hebrews 7:25
Therefore He also is able to save to the uttermost those who come to God through Him, since He always lives to make intercession for them.

Romans 8:26, 27
Likewise the Spirit also helps in our weaknesses. For, we do not know what we should pray for as we ought, but the Spirit Himself makes intercession for us with groanings which cannot be uttered. Now He who searches the hearts knows what the mind of the Spirit is, because He makes intercession for the saints according to the will of God.

Romans 8:34
Who is he who condemns? It is Christ who died, and furthermore is also risen, who is even at the right hand of God, who also makes intercession for us.

If Jesus is our Example, and we see Him bringing our requests before the Father, then we as intercessors need to bring our requests before the Father.

Isaiah 59:16
He saw that there was no man, and wondered that there was no intercessor.

Ezekiel 22:30
"So I sought for a man among them who would make a wall, and stand in the gap before Me on behalf of the land, that I should not destroy it; but I found no one."

The Lord is looking for a man or woman to help stand in the gap on behalf of those they are directed to intercede for. This will avoid difficulties by providing protection to cover and blanket people called to businesses, financial stewardship, and the release of resources through Godly visions for Kingdom purposes. If there is any opposition in these areas, someone needs to carry the responsibility in the spirit of prayer and intercession; and continue to complete these prayer assignments in an ongoing basis.

Intercessors link God's mercy with human needs by providing a prayer shield to protect the work to be done. The importance of intercession speaks volumes. This is evident especially as Christians begin to see the value of prayer and continue to stay in "the Spirit" until a breakthrough occurs that brings great evidence that declares someone is praying!

Pray through until you feel a release! Don't stop short of God's release!

People of prayer become very sensitive to the moving of the Holy Spirit. There is a synergistic operation among seasoned prayer warriors and inter-cessors that is *caught*, as well as *taught*. There are many facets of prayer, including a direction and a flow of prayer. Intercession develops this sensitivity in anyone attempting to obey God and pray.

Corporate Prayer: Unity in Agreement

The prayer of agreement unites all participants together in a group, creating explosive power. Unity and harmony in the Spirit of prayer gets the job done! Prayer agreement works as a continuous battle-ax designed to destroy any assignments to hinder, and to execute and expedite God's plan. One mind and one purpose before God get results! Intercession also unveils areas for us to mature in our relationship with God. There will always be a result that produces success with the agreement of others. We need to get on the "one note" which produces a cadence in the spirit with people agreeing in corporate settings of prayer and release a corporate sound in the spirit.

Notice biblical examples of unity and agreement in prayer:

Acts 1:14
These all continued with one accord in prayer and supplication....

Colossians 4:12
...always laboring fervently for you in prayers, that you may stand perfect and complete in all the will of God.

Psalm 5: 1,2
...give ear to my words O Lord, consider my meditation. Give heed to the voice of my cry, My King and my God for to you I pray.

Let's discuss what corporate prayer can achieve. By establishing a corporate setting and a scheduled time to come together in prayer, a foundation is built. This foundation will support the infrastructure of your entire God-given vision and take it through to completion.

Corporate prayer will also add strength to strength to employ a spiritual covering and protection to all the intricate details of your daily and weekly operations. Not only will it build and produce the vision you're praying for, but it will bring strength and unity to leaders and staff. It will pull people into new levels of spiritual operation, maturity, and accountability.

Personal intercessors will be assigned to you when you pray and ask God for them. You may already have people who pray for you to a certain degree. But you need to establish an inner circle of loyal people dedicated to your vision; people of spiritual substance and discernment who understand the responsibility to pray. These intercessors must be dedicated and consecrated to at least one year of service to your vision.

I am enclosing a letter I wrote to my intercessors asking them to seek God in prayer about dedicating themselves to prayer for this ministry. I suggest you do this also.

As I developed a prayer strategy for this ministry assignment, I called on God to bring in intercessors (Romans 4:17), loyal dedicated people of spiritual substance assigned to this vision for a commitment of one year minimum.

As a result, people actually called me or walked up to tell me they were called to pray for me. Some of them I didn't even know at the time! The Holy Spirit knows who is personally assigned to you. If you are faithful to pray and ask God for intercessors, God will assign them to you.

God is waking up the Christian community to a life of prayer. He wants us to be alert and respond when He calls us to prayer.

To help us be more informed and alert to our times of prayer, we must be able to understand how to address significant structures. The watches of prayer as outlined in this next session will bring enlightenment on how powerful prayer alliances are enforced.

Establishing prayer into four separate prayer "watches" throughout the early morning hours has great significance. Many who have been elected to prayer and intercession have often found that they have been summoned by God to stand on a *Morning Prayer Watch* and have responded to that time of prayer daily. *Obedience* is always the key word. When responding to this a lot of spiritual development and authority is established as you and God form very intimate and strong alliances. Much prophetic information is released from the spirit realm to individuals and strategic leaders. Without this response, significant information cannot be assimilated or released. These are seasons of building much spiritual authority that could not come without this response. Much trusted information is released and processed and a great level of spiritual discernment is deposited.

Habakkuk 2:1
"I will stand at my watch and station myself on the ramparts; I will look to see what he will say to me and what answer I am to give to this complaint."

I believe we need more teaching on prayer watches. Very little has been taught on the subject. A prayer watch establishes those called to protect God's people and to discern situations and receive spiritual knowledge that may be used to run interference against any strongholds, or to release Gods glory and angelic power to be commissioned emissaries of enforcement on how to structure needed knowledge for the release of Godly assignments. As people have responded to become worshipers of God in this assignment, He has wooed us in the night season to minister to Him and His desires so that He may receive His reward. This is a great departure from warring in the second heaven by ministering to the Lord, and being translated by ascending into the third heaven. The Holy Spirit has been our teacher to transition us as we entered into a realm of glory and majesty that provoked the very atmosphere to be permeated with Gods holy presence. This is why there are more divine expressions of the third heaven being tangibly manifested in the earth! People have responded and broken through, and God is rewarding or endorsing these people or situations or corporate groups because He is pleased with their hunger!

It makes a lot of sense to understand the pattern of prayer watches starting from the time people's days slow down until the dawn of early morning. This is derived as the *"watchman on the wall."* In biblical times a city was fortified within a walled area. These were usually quit thick or dense and there were sentries who were employed as watchmen by night, who guarded and protected the city from predatory harm of any kind. These sentries had "gate houses" on the wall and between these gatehouses the sentries attended as they stood or walked their watches where they would be working in three hour increments (I am sure these slots where in small increments to stay alert at night). These were called night watches and were assigned posts.

In **Ezekiel 33:1- 7** I am going to pen right here the sovereign importance of understanding these scriptures about the sobriety of the watchman, and even more sobering the need to obediently respond to the call from God to stand on the watch to which He has called you to. You must obey; it is a mandate, it is not optional!

"And the word of the Lord came to me saying. Son of man, speak to your people the (Israelites captive in Babylon) and say to them. When I bring the sword upon a land and the people of the land take a man from among the man make him their watchman. If when he sees the sword coming upon the land, he blows the trumpet and warns the people. Then whoever hears the sound of trumpet and does not take warning and the sword comes and takes him away his blood is on his own head. He heard the sound of the trumpet and did take warning; his blood shall be upon himself. 'But he who takes warning shall save his life. But if the watchman sees the sword coming and does not blow the trumpet and the people are not warned, and the sword comes and take any one of them he is taken away in and for his perversity and iniquity. But the blood will I require at the watchman's hand. So you, son of man, I have made you a watchman of the house of Israel: therefore hear the word of My mouth and give them warning from Me."

The term "shamar" is frequently used throughout scripture and is the term used in Genesis 2:15 *"Then the Lord God took the man and put him in the garden of Eden to tend and keep it."* The term to "tend and keep" is "shamar" often used for the term *"watch"* biblically. It connotes a highly attentive position towards the "garden" God has given us to tend. <u>To watch</u> is God's first command to man as He created Him. We are therefore all called to *"watch."*

Biblically, the term <u>watch</u>, to see, etc. is used as frequently as prayer, but it connotes a higher level of attentiveness to the issues we are praying about. As we now face the challenges of terrorism, wars, and a fraying of the moral fabric of our nations, God is now restoring prayer watches to our cities to help advance and protect His purposes.

Biblically, the Hebrew watch consisted of three watches, the evening watch, middle watch and morning watch. When the Roman Empire took over, the watches were divided into first-fourth watch in 3 hour segments, 6pm-9pm, 9pm-12am, 12am-3am, and 3am-6am respectively. ***The morning watch or 4th watch in particular scripturally is very significant and much advance can be made when people and groups pray during that time, even with small numbers.***

There is strategic significance in praying during the early morning hours. Prayers during these early morning hours are highly effectual in harnessing God's transforming power.

The fourth watch is defined by the Roman watch as a time spanning from 3am-6am. Biblically, strategic events take place particularly during the night and early morning hours/watches.

- Jacob wrestled with God and met Him face to face just before entering into his destiny as Israel. Genesis 32:22-31
- Moses led the Israelites across the Red Sea Exodus 14:25-26
- Gideon defeated the Midianites, Judges 7:19-24
- Peter and Jesus walk on water, Matthew 14:25-26
- Jesus is resurrected from the dead, Matthew 28:1
- The bridegroom woes His bride in the night hours, Song of Solomon

The Hebrew watch was divided into three watches, the first, middle and morning watch. As the Roman influence and supremacy was established, the number of watches increased to four and were described in numerical order:

- **1st   6pm-9pm**
- **2nd   9pm-12am**
- **3rd   12am-3am**
- **4th   3am-6am.**

During the 4th watch there are significant power encounters that make way for the Kingdom of God to penetrate the earth. Such prayers are highly protective and carry transforming power particularly when linked with other watchmen. The importance to apprehend the purposes of God in prayer during these hours is highly strategic and powerful.

Thus, much advance can be made even with a few people in agreement. Corporate and cooperative prayer during the fourth watch is therefore highly effectual in harnessing God's transforming power for our lives, city, state, and nation.

Furthermore, Jesus' parable of the sower and the seed represents a reflection of Kingdom dynamics. After all, it is Jesus who said *The Kingdom of Heaven is like a man who sowed good seed in his field; but while men slept, his enemy came and sowed tares among the wheat and went his way*. Matthew 13:24-25.

If this is a season of Kingdom advance, perhaps *"fasting" sleep* will not only be powerful but help break spiritual slumber off the "church" so that it can advance into this third reformation in process. The 4th watch is a powerful time of both personal and corporate breakthrough into His presence. God is looking for Samuel's today who will respond to Him when the 3am wake-up call comes by saying, "What is it Lord, here am I." This is not just an idea but a real provoking of the Holy Spirit Himself upon God's people in these days of conflict to bring spiritual breakthrough and Kingdom advance.

As I speak to people, more and more, I ask the question: Is God waking you in the middle of the night?

When God wakes you up, believe me, you won't need an alarm clock! For example, I have been sound asleep, and I've heard what sounds like a telephone, a knock, a bell, or an alarm. I know its God's call for me to get up and pray! Most of the time I just wake up and start preparing to seek God and inquiring in praying what His desire or information for me is to begin the day without any other prompting. He wants to instruct us for this very day! It becomes very familiar the more we respond to His calling.

God wants you positioned and ready for prayer! Are you willing to yield yourself "as a living sacrifice to His reasonable service holy and acceptable," Romans 12:1, surrendering yourself to time with Him? Are you willing to stand for the protection and breakthrough necessary to fulfill your election to walk in Godly prosperity and steward kingdom resources? Are you willing to position yourself for end-time wealth for this great harvest?

Prayer and praise is like fire and incense as we present ourselves in worship and intercession to His Majesty the King of Kings and Lord of Lords, the Most High God.

Allow the Holy Spirit's power to fall and pull out all the stops. Do what He asks, so you can go as His minister into the business arena or marketplace serving financial leaders, impacting lives with the anointing of God! God will fund His Gospel of the Kingdom message and the many projects that need finances through the power of prayer.

Some people are called to sow to your ministry in a spiritual manner or capacity. They are assigned by God as a support team to stand as a shield, a covering, and a bridge to pray for all aspects of your God-given vision. They are brought to you by God as you petition Him in prayer for intercessors called to your ministry. Then begin to call in those people who are assigned to pray for you.

From my own Prayer Strategy for this ministry I will quote:

> *"I call into this business those people aligned to this <u>Your business</u> in me. God, I'm asking You for people of spiritual quality who are in the highest position of prayer. Those called as intercessors, I call them to be faithful prayer warriors (intercessors), calling on God to establish, protect, and provide for every aspect of this <u>Your business.</u>*
> *Father, in the Name of Jesus, The Name above all names, I call faithful, obedient intercessors to come forth. I call forth people of spiritual substance to agree and stand against the powers of darkness and stand to establish your desires for progress daily to protect Ann Bandini, Ann's family and CEO Leadership Consulting and Training Institute."*

You see, your intercessors must be people of "spiritual substance" called forth and given to you by God. Petition Him in prayer, calling in these people assigned by God to pray for you.

You want loyal people who will commit to pray to stand, to birth new areas, to know the seasons they must be called upon to protect you, and to promote a spiritual covering for what God has assigned for you to do in the earth. He will send you intercessors with right motives, spiritual discernment; those who hear the voice of God.

The intercessors God gives you will have a strong call to prayer because they understand that their first ministry is to the Lord. Intercessors are strengthened by continually entering into God's Presence by honoring, submitting, and consecrating themselves to Him.

Worship is the highest form of entering into God's Presence. Worship and praise activates God's angelic forces and releases the power of the Holy Spirit, so that the very spiritual atmosphere is charged and changed. This gives way to the supernatural release of the power of God.

I am reminded of a teaching I recently heard regarding angels. We know the Word says, *"Angels hearken to the voice of God's Word"* Psalm. 103:20-21. *"Bless (affectionately, gratefully praise) the Lord, you His angles, you mighty ones who do His commandments harkening to the voice of His word. Bless (affectionately, gratefully praise) the Lord, all you His hosts, you His ministers who do His pleasure."* This statement alone should compel us to charge the atmosphere audibly with the plans and pursuits of God. This will further excite us and motive the activation of angels working on our behalf.

I don't know if this is a true statement or not, but I heard the following information made regarding the ministry of angels from one of our major Christian leaders. "All people are assigned one legion of angels." In this teachers research they expressed that a legion consists of 6,000 angels per believer.

So we have armies of angelic hosts at our disposal waiting for us to declare and decree God's Word so they can be sent on assignment to perform the will of God. The scripture says angels hearken to God's Word. Furthermore, angels are empowered to guard, protect, and marshal Gods plans and to do warfare in battles in heavenly realms when we stand in faith against Satan, who is a defeated foe. We must decree the Word of God! We have tremendous power to employ, as we declare and decree scriptures with the authority that we have been given.

We enforce Jesus' defeat of the enemy onslaughts as we audibly pray the Word of God with our own mouths. Praying in agreement with our intercessors adds enormous spiritual covering and strength. We can surely do exploits in God, conquering the opposition as we press forward in Christ.

Isaiah 45:11
Thus says the LORD, the Holy One of Israel, and his Maker, Ask me of things to come concerning my sons, and concerning the work of my hands command ye me.

If this angelic army is waiting for our military command based on God's Word, we must understand the power of the word "command." It encompasses the following meanings:

- to direct with specific authority
- to order
- to command troops to march

- to authoritatively demand
- to dominate by reason of location
- to have control over
- to occupy a dominating position

Have you been stirred up to employ all of this supernatural power available to you? Are you provoked enough in God to call forth your intercessors?

Praying in ones prayer language (the spiritual gift of speaking in tongues) is one of the greatest power tools of intercession. It confuses the enemy assignments, you are praying mysteries and you are becoming personally edified, and much is birthed into the Kingdom of God by activating and utilizing this gift. Praying in tongues is a powerful tool for intervention in the realm of the spirit.

God is shifting our level of prayer. Many times we can go deeper by employing the sound of the spirit which is a primordial call, crying out to God in desperation for breaking all the way through in challenging circumstances. This is a deep cry from the depth of the center of our spirits, which connects us spirit to spirit to the conditions at hand! Boldly crying out! As "the whole earth is crying for the redemption of the sons of men." This breaks apart major resistance!

Praying in the Spirit or praying in tongues will break down strongholds. It helps you tap into the revelations of God. Your intercessors will be seasoned prayer warriors prepared to pay the price to do go deep in God at all cost.

Your Intercessors will have compelling prayer lives and operate in many spiritual gifts. They will be faithful to discern and pray through until there is a release for your plan to come forth in the Spirit. Your God-given intercessors will know when the manifestation of their prayers has broken through. The breakthrough will come with a sense of victory. Intercessors are very sensitive to the workings of the Holy Spirit.

As you and your intercessors pray, there is continual strength for your spiritual position over your assignments. You will continue to rise to a higher dimension spiritually. You will be released from strongholds that use to sap your time, energy, health, and resources. You will feel an ease over areas that have been resistant.

As the intercessors pray, you will actually understand more about the corporate team who are assigned to pray for you and how it continues to affect your progress

I heard a prominent spiritual leader at a conference state: "We don't need more money; we need more prayer!" This leader was saying that money is secondary, but prayer is of the utmost importance. Actually, money will come when our priorities are on praying and seeking God.

The following is a letter I composed for my intercessors:

The Lord has revealed to me the information I am enclosing in this letter to you.

Would you please take the time to carefully read its contents? This is a very pivotal time for the national and international launching of this ministry. I need to ask you to make a commitment to become an intercessor for a period of one year.

I need you to prepare yourselves by seeking God before you make this decision. I can't tell you how important this will be to the success, and the doors of the ministry opportunity opening up so that the gift of God in me will be established in the earth.

I need specific Corporate Consecration to Christ's Exceeding Opportunities Ministries. Will you dedicate yourself, committing to this God-given cause?

Commitment:

1. To give in trust or charge
2. To pledge or engaging oneself
3. To obligate someone to do something
4. To promise or commission
5. To bind
6. To allot for a certain purpose
7. To assign

Please know how important you are in prayer. You are of great value to this ministry as you commit to this assignment in God.

Your dedication to this purpose and your specific involvement and application to this ministry is noted by God in Heaven. Your prayer commitment will release the anointing and touch thousands for Christ.

Exodus 19:22
Also let the priests who come near the Lord sanctify themselves, lest the Lord break out against them.

Isaiah 63:5
I looked but there was no one to help, and I wondered that there was no one to uphold.

Isaiah 59:16
He saw that there was no man, and wondered that there was no intercessor.

As we approach our future in God, we are sober regarding the anointing that must be carried to the world. The reverential awe or fear of our Creator strengthens our resolve to please Him, motivating us to persuade others to trust in Jesus Christ.

Therefore, I spend time in dedication and consecration asking the Lord to assign you to this very important task. I can't do this without your support in prayer. There are no words to describe how valuable your prayers are.

I will be sending you the weekly prayer sheet enclosed for your time with the Lord. I *will be asking on occasion for greater prayer covering as I travel and go out to minister.*

Thank you on behalf of all the people you will be sending me to by your prayer covering. Thank you on behalf of the anointing God has poured into me. Thank you on behalf of my daughter (for keeping me protected). I appreciate you beyond measure. You are the most important part of this ministry. Without prayer it can't exist.

In His exciting service,
Ann Bandini

Chapter 9

HOW TO EXECUTE A STRATEGIC PRAYER PLAN

In order to set in motion your vision and fulfill your dream, a plan of action must be set in place. How are your dreams and visions brought into reality? How is a spiritual plan developed properly? How can you make the dream of your heart a reality?

One way to make your dreams a reality is by executing a strategic prayer plan. The word "execute" means to accomplish or carry out a specific plan. It means to complete or fulfill something.

For example, in the natural realm look at what makes a successful businessperson. Education and training play a part in every businessperson's success. And the world has always tried to dictate what would make us successful by making us think human effort alone brought success.

And in the past, most of us have probably followed a natural path of progress and success based on knowledge and training. And that's fine to a point. However, God by His Holy Spirit wants to train us differently by adding the dimension of the miraculous to our success. He wants to release into our lives a dynamic spiritual plan that will make our visions and dreams successful in Him.

Actually, there's not much teaching that shows us how to apply God's Word to develop a personal format of prayer for our business endeavors. There has not been a concise, specific training to show us how to set God's spiritual plan in motion for our lives.

Gods design by the inspiration of the Holy Spirit is to give each person specific instructions how to develop their own business plan—spiritually and in the natural.

In order to develop with the natural understanding or to establish, and execute any business venture, great planning and details must be put into the planning stages. Graphs, budgets and calculations are made; cost and financial evaluations are analyzed; deadlines, timelines and projections are established; and projected goals are all written out in precise detail.

Everything is accounted for with impeccable maneuvering. When all of this groundwork is finally meticulously laid out, a wise businessperson forges ahead, armed with a developed, detailed business plan. Now he is ready to accomplish with great success the inspiration of his heart and the gifting for which he was created by God to produce.

In light of this, let me ask you some questions. Have you considered starting your business venture? Are you currently in an established business? If so, do you have a prayer plan equal to your business plan? Have you sought God through prayer for His plans for your business? Have you thought about going to God to seek Him about how to develop a detailed prayer strategy to ensure the success of your business? Is this a new and unusual concept for you? If so, in this chapter we are going to give you concise information on how to do just that. These details will help you be the creator of your own personal plan of action.

God has the power to help you develop a strategy exclusively for the success of your business. The word "strategy" means a careful plan or method. It also means the art of directing large-scale military movements or operations. In today's business world and volatile economy, we need to be prepared with spiritual maneuvers much like the expertise of military personnel.

A prayer strategy is a spiritual prayer plan. It is your God given, written document, a "blueprint" if you will, to be used as a spiritual tool, to vocally establish your own prophetic proclamation of His Word over the execution of your financial assignment. The use of this tool will establish His ongoing strategy to assist in the continued execution of His Kingdom plan.

The Holy Spirit is our wonderful Teacher. He guides us. He will show us the power of the Word to develop our business in the realm of the spirit. Establishing our business takes on an empowered dimension as we seek the counsel of the Holy Spirit.

The Holy Spirit leads us as our Teacher and business Mentor into the scriptures that will impact our progress. When we apply God's Word to our business successes, the Word begins to come alive on a very personal level. When we petition God in prayer using His Word, we are giving birth to what we desire, hope for, and expect. A prayer "strategy" is needed to proclaim God's plan of action daily in and over our businesses. This tool can be used by others who are assigned and commissioned to pray for the success of your enterprise.

The building blocks for developing your business prayer strategy are the promises of God that ensure your success and even wealth. They are just waiting for you to extract them from the Bible.

For example, it is very enlightening to be led by the Holy Spirit to a scripture or several scriptures, ensuring your success. Then as you write them out and make them part of your spiritual "tools," you are actually orchestrating the infrastructure of a powerful financial declaration that will enable God to successfully guide you into the arena of financial success.

Just as God imparted the knowledge revealing what you are called to do, He will also lead in every aspect of establishing your business financially. He will do this by giving you a definite prayer strategy. The challenge is to write down the blueprint. We will show you a physically structured prayer strategy in this chapter. In other words, write down your business prayer needs and establish them on the promises in God's Word. Then you must lay the foundation to build the cornerstone of a prayer strategy.

Webster's dictionary defines "cornerstone" as a stone uniting two masonry walls at an intersection. A stone represents a nominal starting place in the construction of a monumental building. A cornerstone is the foundation on which something is constructed or built.

In this book, we've discussed at length how to develop a life of prayer—and ways to seek God. Developing a business prayer strategy will begin much the same way. God has much to reveal to us as we seek Him for His plan for our financial success.

Realize that a *business prayer strategy* is very personal; God will guide you to tailor-make it to your own business endeavor. We are all creative and different in approaching our dreams. God knows that. Therefore, He knows just what He wants to reveal to us through His Word. He just asks us to come to Him, so He can reveal His exact plan for assisting our financial foundation and expansion for each one of us.

As we spend time creating an atmosphere for God to respond, His power begins to invade our prayer time with Him. Expect to hear from God! Expect Him to reveal His plan to you! Developing your spirit so that you can hear God's response is not difficult. But it is very precious and personal. He responds when we are seeking Him because He knows we need His word as our guide in all of our endeavors:

> **Psalm 119:105**
> *Your word is a lamp to my feet and a light to my path.*

God's Word is your source to guide, teach, correct, instruct, lead, and confirm all the details in developing your business prayer strategy. This business prayer strategy will be a powerful prayer tool given to you by Him alone. By praying, your faith, knowledge and authority from God's Word out loud, you will declare and decree His assignments into the natural and spiritual atmosphere to set in motion activity in heaven to expedite all the plans God has given to you to accomplish.

You may ask yourself, "So how do I go about developing a business prayer strategy?" Or more specifically, "how do I go about writing out a business prayer strategy?" In order to write a prayer strategy, first gather the following study tools together. This is similar to what we have previously discussed in becoming a student of God's Word.

THE SAME APPLICATION AND EXAMPLES OF WHAT YOU WILL NEED FOLLOWS:

1. A good study Bible
My favorite is the *Spirit Filled Life Bible*.

2. The Amplified Bible

I like *The Amplified Bible* because it truly helps deliver more detail and gives a greater variety of expression. It's also helpful to study differences in scriptural passages from other translations.

3. A Dictionary

You will want a computer program of the following, or a Webster's dictionary, plus a good Bible dictionary.

4. A Concordance

A computer program of, *Strong's Exhaustive Concordance* gives you all the scripture references for every word you desire to study in the Bible. Or the book form of *Strong's Exhaustive Concordance*

5. Computer Software

Or you can have your favorite computer program of Bible software or a computer program of all of these study tools as well.

6. Paper for Notes

Last you will want a legal pad; a notebook; a journal or your personal PC to do your journaling or personal recording in.

Armed with these "tools," you are now ready to embark on a tremendous spiritual journey. Once you have gathered all your study tools, you may then want to prepare yourself spiritually. Preparing yourself spiritually will probably include finding an appropriate time to seek the Lord, as well as creating the proper spiritual atmosphere to seek Him.

In order to give your full attention to study, you need to select a time of day when you are separated from all the distractions that would pull you away from your focus. You must find a time that will be most comfortable to achieve success and progress.

As a student of God's Word, you need to create the environment of a student. And just as a businessman prepares for an important presentation or seminar; you will also need an environment conducive to this type of preparation.

Since God is your Teacher by His Holy Spirit, and since He is the CEO of all your business endeavors, you want to approach Him and submit yourself to Him for His direction and counsel.

I would even suggest that you bring worship CD's and a CD player or your MP3 player to your time of study and preparation. First before anything else, give God the place of adoration with submission in worship. Then the atmosphere created will electrify with spontaneity and release the tremendous power and knowledge God wants to present to you.

Once you've brought the Presence of the Lord into your study and preparation time, begin to ask the Holy Spirit (as your Mentor) to teach you, direct you, and guide you.

He will begin to speak to you, perhaps by just giving you one scripture or one Book of the Bible to study—or even one chapter! Or He will lead you on a particular word study. Follow God's leading in your studying. When you read these chapters' verses or a word theme, you will find they are exactly what you need. They'll come alive with substance and anointing!

Write out these verses. Check the cross-referenced scriptures in the margins of your Study Bible. Write out the cross references also. You may need to check your concordance to find additional compatible scripture references. Write these out and add as needed to the mix. Look through the foot notes for additional information and in most Study Bibles there are other study modalities that will take you to places in the Bible to give additional insights to the specifics of what you are learning to study.

As you begin to become a student in all of this you will become transformed in the process because you have been deeply searching the word as directed by God to give you so much revealed truth in many needed areas

You may notice that words within these scriptures just begin to jump out at you or become emphasized in your spirit. Look up these words in the dictionary and write out their meanings. You may want to look at *The Amplified Bible* as well and see how these words or scriptures are expressed there with many synonyms added.

This is how you begin to hear God's Word for you personally. By focusing your prayer and study on building business success, you are actually developing and building the foundation and infrastructure of a prayer strategy. Developing a prayer strategy takes time. It's not something you can rush through. It is a significant and wonderfully designed spiritual prayer tool given just to you by God alone.

Some prayer strategies have taken me several days of praying and studying before God to put them together. I had to be fully committed to their development. This should never be something to just rush through.

Once this strategy is produced, it will be your vision in a divinely inspired spiritual format/document. This is now your personal declaration and prophetic statement. Your own strategy and tool.

Once you receive God's Word for your particular business endeavor, you will use His Word to daily decree His plan of success over your business vision. The following are some scriptures you can use as your prayer foundation.

Job 22:28
You will also declare a thing and it will be established for you; so light will shine on your ways. "

Jeremiah 23:29
Is not My word like a fire [that consumes all that cannot endure the test]? says the Lord, and like a hammer that breaks in pieces the rock [of most stubborn resistance].

2 Corinthians 10:4,5
For the weapons of our warfare are not carnal but mighty in God for pulling down strongholds. Casting down imaginations and every high thing that exalts itself against the

knowledge of God, bringing every thought into captivity to the obedience of Christ.

This prayer strategy will empower you to break-through personal strongholds and remove all fleshly distractions which are in opposition to the coming glory of God's will in your business and financial assignment. You are about to see the power of your words linked with the power of God's Word explode into your business atmosphere and financial endeavors.

Here is one of the greatest scriptures to express why a strategy of prayer will empower and power-fully influence you:

Habakkuk 2:1
I will stand my watch and set myself on the rampart, and watch to see what He will say to me.

The word "watch" means to look attentively to see what is done or what happens. It is being attentive and expectant, yet careful and cautious. It also means to keep a vigil for devotional purposes, looking out and guarding you in preparation with a word specifically for you.

Habakkuk 2:2,3
Then the Lord...said: "Write the vision and make it plain on tablets, that he many run who reads it. For the vision is yet for an appointed time; but at the end it will speak,

and it will not lie. Though it tarries, wait for it; because it will surely come. It will not tarry."

You won't be able to write the vision and make it plain, if you haven't set aside a time and place to commune with God, pray, and listen for His specific scriptures and instructions to produce a spiritual document given to you by Him! We can tell from this passage of scripture that Habakkuk has routinely set aside appointed times to listen to the Lord.

As you meet with God, you will find that inspiration will begin to pour through you by reading, meditating, and writing down God's vision. God's detailed plan for you will pour forth from the heart of God as you commune with Him. Ask the Holy Spirit to guide you in this as it is His job to mentor and instruct you.

Your God-given vision is a written substance that will enlighten all of the people who read it; they will "catch the vision" as they feel and receive the anointing from this document of prayer. The scriptures God gives you are His plan written plainly. By applying the scriptures God gives you, He has assisted and directed you to write the vision and making it plain for you and those who pray for you to read and run with it!

As you begin to proclaim God's Word over your business, you will notice that you are able to move quite freely without restraints. Those who are assigned to pursue prayer on your behalf will experience the same thing. They will begin to run, to chase, and to pursue the vision that God's given you.

When we have dealt with issues of the heart and become sanctified for service, God is releasing us to meditate and "work the Word of God" so to speak, by proclaiming it over our divinely appointed projects. It is at this juncture that we will be released into financial service and be able to accomplish what He's asked us to do. The finances will come forth to support the work of the Gospel of the Kingdom. As we pray, God will fund our part of the Great Commission!

People will be brought out of their world of sin and confusion into their eternal destiny of salvation in the Lordship of Jesus Christ. They will walk in total deliverance. We truly are a privilege people because we serve a Mighty God.

I have included a prayer strategy I developed. It took me two days to pray, write, and complete this particular prayer strategy, but it will provide you an example to use for your own business.

PRAYER STRATEGY FOR BUSINESS

Father, I petition You for success of myself and for all whom You bring to me for mutual benefit in this business opportunity. I bring Your own Word to You because I am standing on Your promises to me.

Jeremiah 23:29
Is not My word like a fire [that consumes all that cannot endure the test]? says the Lord,

and like a hammer that breaks in pieces the rock [of most stubborn resistance]?

Therefore, I boldly speak forth Your Word over this business opportunity, expelling any resistance in the Name of Jesus.

I ask You to build my business on a firm foundation so that all who join me in it are solid in their commitment to succeed according to godly principles.

Matthew 7:24
...a sensible (prudent, practical, wise) man [is one] who built his house upon the rock. (Amplified Bible)

Hebrews 11:10
For he was waiting expectantly and confidently, looking forward to the city which has fixed and firm foundations, whose Architect and Builder is God. (Amplified Bible)

By building my financial success on God's Word, I am making Him my Architect and Master Builder. So my business is actually built by God!

2 Timothy 2:19
But the firm foundation of [laid by] God stands, sure and unshaken, bearing this seal (inscription): "The Lord knows those who are His...." (Amplified Bible)

Father, as I continue to speak forth Your word with boldness according to the following scriptures, I will expect to see massive changes in my business:

Psalm 138:2
I will worship toward Your holy temple, and praise Your name for Your loving-kindness and for Your truth and faithfulness; for You have exalted above all else Your name and Your word, and YOU HAVE MAGNIFIED Your word above all Your name!

Psalm 1:3
And...[I] shall be like a tree firmly planted [and tended] by the streams of water, ready to bring forth his fruit in its season; his leaf also shall not fade or wither, and everything...[I] do shall prosper and come to maturity. (Amplified Bible)

Jeremiah 17:7, 8
[Most] blessed is the man [and woman] who believes in, trusts in, and relies on the Lord, and whose hope and confidence the Lord is. For he [or she] will be like a tree planted by the waters, and spreads out its roots by the river, and shall not see and fear when heat comes; but his leaf shall be green; he shall not be anxious and careful in the year of drought, nor shall he cease from yielding fruit. (Amplified Bible)

My financial success in business is totally dependent upon seeking the Lord. The wealth that is given for me to steward will only occur as I spend time in His Presence, worshipping Him and speaking forth His Word boldly. His anointed Word releases all God's provisions that belong to me.

As I petition for business contacts before the Lord, I will not approach my circumstances in the flesh, but I will accomplish all things by power of the Spirit of God.

Lord, according to Isaiah 43:26, Your Word says I am to put You in remembrance of Your Word.

Isaiah 43:26
Put Me in remembrance—remind Me of your merits; let us plead and argue together. Set forth my case, that I may be justified—proved in the right!

Father, I put You in remembrance of Your Word. Father, I sow forth these scriptures as seed. I sow all the scriptures in this prayer strategy to bring forth the harvest. By doing so, I am changing the course of my life, because Your word is imperishable seed sown. It is sprouting and increasing supernaturally. I ask for wisdom, discernment, and new revelations.

Proverbs 1:5
The wise also may hear and increase in learning, and the person of understanding acquire skill and attain to sound counsels

[so that he may be able to steer his course rightly].

Proverbs 9:9
Give instruction to a wise man, and he will be yet wiser; teach a righteous man—one upright and in right standing with God—and he will increase in learning.

To establish spiritual authority for this business opportunity, I decree the following:

I will pray daily to break open this territory and all additional places that I may have business contacts for this program. I will rise early to pray and commune with my Lord:

Psalm 5:3
In the morning You hear my voice, O Lord; in the morning I prepare [a prayer, a sacrifice] for You, and watch and wait [for You to speak to my heart].

John 1:51
Then He said to him, I assure you, most solemnly I tell you all, you shall see Heaven opened up, and the angels of God ascending and descending upon the Son of Man!

I decree an open heaven over this business in each territory. I speak forth my faith boldly, and I decree protection based on Your Word.

Luke 10:19
Behold! I have given you authority and power to trample upon serpents and scorpions, and (physical and mental strength and ability) over all the power that the enemy [possesses], and nothing shall in any way harm you.

Heavenly Father, I prepare for and expect Your divine appointments spiritually and professionally each day:

Proverbs 16:9
A man's mind plans his way, but the Lord directs his steps and makes them sure.

I declare and decree daily assignments for prosperity:

Daniel 11:32
...but the people who know their God shall prove themselves strong and shall stand firm, and do exploits [for God].

I am desperate to *know* You, God. In knowing You, You will reveal to me ways to prosper my business:

Jeremiah 33:3
Call to Me and I will answer you and show you great and mighty things, fenced in and hidden, which you do not know—do not

distinguish and recognize, have knowledge of and understand.

Heavenly Father, Lord Jesus, and precious Holy Spirit my Comforter and Guide, I speak forth your supernatural favor.

Psalm 90:17
Let the beauty and delightfulness and favor of the Lord our God be upon us; confirm and establish the work of our hands, yes, the work of our hands, confirm and establish it.

Exodus 3:21
"And I will give favor in the sight of (his/her business); and it shall be when he/she goes that he/she shall not go empty handed."

Exodus 12:36
"And the Lord has given me favor in the sight of (by business opportunities), so that they granted him/her what she requested. Thus she plundered her enemies."

Deuteronomy 33:23
"As my business is satisfied with favor and full of the blessing of the Lord! Possessing the west and the south!"

I bind any spiritual or natural backlash, retaliation, witchcraft, and hindrances directed toward your original plans and final outcome based on Your Words in the authority of the Name of Jesus.

Matthew 16:19
I will give you the keys of the kingdom of heaven, and whatever you bind—that is, declare to be improper and unlawful—on earth must be what is already bound in heaven; and whatever you loose—declare lawful—on earth must be what is already loosed in heaven.

Heavenly Father, I will cooperate with Your divine order.

Philippians 3:16
Only let us hold true to what we have already attained and walk and order our lives by that.

2 Chronicles 27:6
So Jotham grew mighty, for he ordered his ways in the sight of the Lord his God.

As I seek You, Lord, and pray Your Word over this business opportunity, I do not keep silent until great prosperity is established in the spiritual realm. I plead my case that I may be justified.

Jeremiah 1:12
Then said the Lord to me, You have seen well, for I am alert and ACTIVE, watching over My word to perform it.

Isaiah 55:11
So shall My word be that goes forth out of My mouth; it shall not return to Me void— without producing any effect, useless—but it shall accomplish that which I please and purpose, and it shall prosper in the thing for which I sent it.

Deuteronomy 29:9
Therefore keep the words of this covenant and do them, that you may deal wisely and prosper in all that you do.

I am changing the course of my life by praying your Word God.

Psalm 147:15
He sends forth His commandment to the earth; His word runs VERY SWIFTLY.

The word "swiftly" means capable of moving with great speed or velocity; coming, happening, or performed quickly or without delay; quick to act or respond.

So according to Psalm 147:15 I decree my God and His Word is capable of moving with great speed and velocity. My business is coming together quickly without delay. My God is making it happen and is quick to act and respond.

Isaiah 53:12
And He shall divide the spoil with the mighty, because He poured out His life unto death.

Lord Jesus, as You poured out Your life unto death, I ask You to count me worthy to carry a great financial call, prospering not for selfish gain, but to advance Your Kingdom. But no matter what my financial state may be, I will always desperately need You. May I always fulfill Your plans for me to be a channel of finances to fund the end-time harvest!

Chapter 10

PROTECTION AND SAFETY ABIDING IN GOD'S PRESENCE

People are being called, activated, and dispatched into the area of financial stewardship and the release of Kingdom wealth and resources. Therefore, understanding God's divine protection is very important because of the subtle attacks against believers' who are assigned to steward wealth. There are the appearances of many external "enemies" in the form of soul restoration, and much allowable refinement by God for true Kingdom financiers. Those who are elected and called to the assignment to be distributors and stewards of wealth will encounter many seasons of preparation. It is during these times that much character development is going to take place, and, of course, there is the endurance to prevail which will cost more in the areas of brokenness, humility, and submission. At times it will feel as if it is more than we envisioned we would endure through this training process. And God will put his fingerprints on the things we never knew were in us!

And very often people called into a business/ministry assignment to prepare for finances and stewarding wealth, will go through much personal death to self and sometimes even separation from material possessions. This process, although unnerving at times, often signals a season of preparation and training by God for total dependence upon Him to create the streams of wealth and business direction soverignly.

During each juncture on the road of refinement where God takes *materialism* out of our hearts, (which is translated into the principality of "mammon", or the love of money (a focus in western thinking) we are put through tests of obedience and sometimes we even suffer extreme personal sacrifice and losses. As this journey continues, we begin to understand in deeper measures of the leading of God to become totally, and desperately dependent on Him.

Oftentimes we are profoundly "stretched" as God commands us out of the "boat of complacency" and onto the water, so to speak, beckoning us to progressively come just a little bit further in our spiritual growth than we have ever before exercised *the gift of faith*. As we grow, we gain greater and greater trust of God's leading. Each time we come out of our comfort zone just a little bit more, sometimes perhaps more than we even desire—but it's for our ultimate benefit, and we will need the endurance for the demands ahead as we learn to hear His voice accurately.

We must always learn to be led by the Spirit of God, especially in the area of responsible steward-ship of what He is about to entrust to us. It is times like these that we begin to understand the reveren-tial fear of a Holy God. Without that sobering rever-ence for this assignment we can swiftly be caught up in the seduction of financial success and what it represents. This is why God allows us to become dependant on Him alone. "Money" of its own is not a self-consumptive commodity or physical entity of our assignment! Money as a tool for serving God in a Holy election or calling, it is neutral.

Let's face it, sometimes comfort is a luxury on this journey that we cannot afford! At times, God takes us out of our comfort zones so that He can do much needed realignment or work in us. If we'll *just trust Him*, we will become use to the changes all around and learn to look to Him alone. We can enter into times when we feel like a reproach and a contra-diction! We must patiently let God work everything out according to His original plan!

Often on the journey you will receive prophetic words of confirmation, or spoken impartations, which are trumpeted into the atmosphere confirming what your assignment is to be established in the earth. And this will be an acknowledgement of why you were created! Many don't know the duality of this. One, it is the confirmation of what God has already deposited into your spirit and understanding to punctuate that you are hearing God correctly and it is His endorsement. The other is this may be the *last good day you will have for awhile*, because now there is a war in the heavens to establish a season of training and refinement and the time has begun for much transition! These words have weight and must be prayed out faithfully to charge the atmosphere with the ability to break through. Often the opposition will be excruciating! But with each challenge we are learning to walk as an over-comer.

Another thing is to seek understanding from God for the next level of direction on how these prophetic words are to play out in a three to five year window of preparation, on behalf of the prophetic words coming into manifestation with substance.

1 Timothy 1:18
"This charge and admonition I commit in trust to you. Timothy, my son, in accordance with prophetic intimations which I formerly received concerning you so that inspired and aided by them you may wage the good warfare."

During these times of change, we need to focus on the excitement of our training adventure in God's army, not the hardships! This is a time to learn about how God is developing new mind sets, releasing us from old traditions. He introduces us to institute spiritual equipment, such as the armor of God and how to tap into God's supernatural protection and the release of angelic activity; the sounds of heaven, and all that is available to assist us to produce what God has assigned us to do.

Most business people are in a hurry, but through the process of learning to depend on God, we are forced to slow down. Sometimes God has to get our attention. And we must choose our time with Him wisely, because we can't afford to skip the details and not discern things through the spirit realm so that we don't head off in the business world unprotected and ill equipped.

By now you have learned through your experiences that your priorities must always begin with intimacy and continual communication with God! In all that you have learned so far, we continue to punctuate that your first priority is to desire the Lord's presence with all of your heart at the beginning of your day.

Realize that in your times of prayer with God, He has positioned Himself as your Senior Partner in all of your dealings—both business and financial. Therefore, your first concern is to maintain an intimate communion with the one I call the CEO of the Universe!

Then your second concern is to be knowledgeable about personal choices that may be tests. Realize that there are assignments and tests along the way to determine the ability to grow in your authority and integrity in times of stretching. You have attained an unsolicited place in the fires of affliction at times. Your work in God's Kingdom represents multitudes of saved souls, provision for hurting humanity in areas of depravation, and emergency responses as a world in turmoil is in need of your obedience. There are people at the end of your obedience waiting to fulfill their destinies! Will you pay the price and respond? Will you obey?

This refinement comes to add necessary strength for the assignment. This is why you've crossed many financial barriers, and with each release of God's wealth or provision to you, the finances will be funneled back into the Kingdom of God. The training is to overcome the enemy of your soul, (mind will and emotions), who knows that you will be a financial support to businesses, the youth who are being raise up; national and international missions, all types of evangelism, prophetic ministries, apostolic works, workplace movements and many other ministry assignments and actions of compassion. And of course, one area so close to my heart, those who are at one of the highest levels of ministry, intercessors and ministers of prayer.

You will be walking in prophetic evangelism among your spheres of influence and be able to interpret things that you see in the spirit realm. You will be given specific dreams, words of knowledge, words of wisdom and interpretation of others dreams. You will begin to be the answer to others prayers in your daily experiences. You will begin to step up into the miraculous and walk in signs and wonders. As the release comes there has been an established strength of discernment, and discerning of spirits that will give circumspect wisdom and focus to be Gods stewards led by Him alone.

As you prosper in business and in your prayer life, you are literally helping to implement deliverance and freedom for many. But don't think you have arrived at this level without being the object of further conflict. It's not that simple. That is why this chapter is very important to be instructed in Godly protection.

Over a process of time, I have had contact with different, highly successful, highly profiled people in financial arenas whose companions or family members have been attacked with terminal diseases. You see the tests that are sent to us can come at an inopportune time. We frustrate the places of darkness and evil forces. We must stand our ground and overcome every obstacle (John 10:10).

Therefore, to succeed and be protected in the financial arena, not only must you maintain a strong prayer life, but you must be faithfully committed to God. You must know how to circumvent opposing forces or evil attacks!

Are You Dressed Like a Spiritual Terminator?

There will be evil testings sent as an onslaught against those believers who give financially into the Kingdom of God. Because of that, Psalm 91 and Ephesians 6:10-18 must be some of the constant scriptural weapons you employ, study, meditate on and decree in prayer these words of life and additional scriptures given to you by God to mediate on. We know our protection from God is based on His Word and we know the final outcome.

Let's look at some key words in scriptures that are crucial to your understanding and protection.

Ephesians 6:10
Finally, my brethren be strong in the Lord and in the power of His might.

Revelations 3: 10- 1
"Because you have guarded and kept My word of patient endurance (have held fast the lesson of My patience with expectant endurance that I give you), I also will keep you (safe) from the hour of trial (testing) which is coming on the whole world to try those who dwell upon the earth. I am coming quickly; hold fast what you have, so that no one may rob you and deprive you of your crown; He who overcomes (is victorious). I will make him a pillar in the sanctuary of My God; he shall never be put out to it or go out of it and I will write him the name of My God an the name of the city of My God, the New Jerusalem, which descends of My God out of heaven and my own new name He who can hear, let him listen to and heed what the spirit of says to the assemblies." (Amplified Bible)

The word "power" means: having the ability to do or act; the capability of doing or accomplishing something; a great or marked ability, strength, might, or force.

Power includes: the possession of control or command over others, it means ascendancy, delegated authority, being strong, capable, confident, or powerful in a specific field or respect.

It is also defined as: a great moral power, firmness, courage; or powerful in influence or authority. The word "mighty" means possessing a superior power or strength.

Ephesians 6:11
Put on the whole armor of God that you may be able to stand against the wiles of the devil.

The word "armor" is defined as any covering worn as a defense against weapons; a protective covering of metal. And armor consists of any quality, characteristic, situation, or thing that serves as protection.

The verb "to stand" means to be in an upright position on one's feet; to take a position as indicated; to adhere to a certain policy or attitude. It also means to endure or withstand; to be conspicuous or prominent; to defend or support; to encounter or fearlessly confront.

The word "wiles" means a trick, artifice, or strategy meant to fool; to trap or entice; an artful or beguiling behavior. It also means deceitful, cunning trickery; to beguile, lure, or entice.

Ephesians 6:12
For we do not wrestle against flesh and blood, but against principalities, against

powers, against the rulers of darkness in this age; against spiritual hosts of wickedness in heavenly places.

Colossians 2:15
Having disarmed principalities and powers, He made a spectacle of them, triumphing over them in it.

The word "disarmed" means to deprive of a weapon or weapons; attack or defense; to deprive; to relieve of hostility; to lay down weapons; to reduce; to limit the size of equipment.

The word "principalities" means a state ruled by a prince; the position or authority of a prince; the rule of a prince.

The word "powers" often means a deity; divinely or heavenly point; the possession of control or command over others; authority or ascendancy; legal ability; capacity, or authority. It also means a person or thing who exercises authority or influence.

Our greatest struggles in business and mammon reft societies in our lives are not against flesh and blood. The footnote on this verse in the Spirit-Filled Life Bible states: "One of the "church's" greatest commands is to discern between the spiritual struggles and other personal and political difficulties. Otherwise individual believers or groups become too easily detoured, wrestling with human adversaries instead of prayerfully taking authority against the invisible works of hell behind the scenes."

The term "heavenly places" recalls earlier references to the following:

1. Spiritual resources available to the church (Ephesians 1:21).
2. The Church is *seated together with our ascended Lord* (Ephesians 2:6).
3. The Father's will displays His wisdom to the Ecclesia; to the confounding of evil powers (Ephesians 3:10).

On these grounds, this passage of scripture announces the believers' corporate assignment to prayer rising above all opposing forces in order to demonstrate the authority that we walk in and advance the will of God.

Ephesians 6:14-18
Stand therefore, having girded your waist with truth, having put on the breastplate of righteousness, and having shod your feet with the preparation of the gospel of peace; above all, taking the shield of faith with which you will be able to quench all the fiery darts of the wicked one. And take the helmet of salvation, and the sword of the Spirit, which is the Word of God; praying always with all prayer and supplication in the Spirit, being watchful to this end with all perseverance and supplication for all the saints.

The armor of God is to be used as a significant truth as each piece is revealed to you. Right now I want you to stop and ask the Holy Spirit, your Teacher and Guide, to give you the personal revelation and truth about God's protection through His armor. Ask Him to open up your spiritual understanding so you can absorb what He has really provided you as one form of protection.

Some of your God given endowments are as follows and allow you to search His word daily for them in an in depth meaning and personal application. These can take you into some exciting studies now that you have had much previous instruction on how to do that in things that have been written in other chapters.

I encourage you to personally seek from God in your own times of study with Him to better understand their meaning in application to your current season:

1. Truth
2. Righteousness
3. Preparation
4. Peace
5. Faith
6. Salvation
7. The Word
8. Prayer
9. Supplication
10. Perseverance

It is your own responsibility now to seek God for the meanings of these ten key words taken from these scriptures in Ephesians on God's spiritual armor and protection. I encourage you to be willing to be a good student of the Word and do individual word studies on these specific words for the opposition that challenges or faces you during these times. With this discipline you will be empowered to be able to sustain the financial anointing God has ordained for you to carry with strength. Now is a good time for you to cloth yourself with the full armor of God daily.

Search the Word of God with *passion*. Let the excitement of your time with God expand your boundaries. You are on an assignment to get the Gospel of the Kingdom preached. You are an extremely important person assigned as Gods partner and leader in the Kingdom. You have been sought out and handpicked by the Lord to pour enormous amounts of resources into the salvation of souls. How wonderful that you are positioned and activated to receive financial wealth!

— Now let's build our spiritual capacity and breakthrough! Let's get going!

PRAYER STRATEGY FOR THE PROTECTION OF HEALTH

Clearly the Lord showed me a need for daily protection of health for people called to the ministry of finance, wealth, and the gift of giving into the end-time harvest. Those anointed in these areas need to discern the assignments that will try to impede or stop the flow of money.

Seek protection and longevity against premature death and destruction by the authority of God's Word. Declaration or decrees by the words of your own mouth are keys to our success. Our words are very weighty when you understand the power of words! This is the very essence of God speaking and permeating existence with the power of His words. Lets look at the profound revelation of what God spoke at the very beginning in the following scripture.

> **Genesis 1:2-5**
> *"When the earth was without form or void and darkness was on the face of the deep and the Spirit of God was hovering over the face of the waters. Then God said, 'Let there be light; and there was light' And God saw the light it was good; and God divided the light from the darkness."*

— Next let us look at understanding the power of daily communion as added to your business and financial assignment for physical strength.

UNDERSTANDING THE MYSTERIES OF TAKING DAILY COMMUNION FOR HEALTH LONGEVITY AND PROTECTION

We must know the appropriation of the mysteries of daily communion for strength and added supernatural physical vitality. By this supernatural expression

Matt 17:

190

we enter into sovereign "protection" which is able to be a defense and is meant to guard from attack, invasion or loss while covering and shielding us.

Matthew 26: 26-28
And as they where eating, Jesus took bread blessed, and broke it, and gave it to the disciples and said, "Take, eat: this is My body,"

And then He took the cup and gave thanks and gave it to them saying; "Drink from it all of you, "For this is my blood of the New Covenant which is shed for many for the remission of sins."

THE LASTING VALUE OF COMMUNION
— By Wade Taylor

As the "facets" in a diamond are viewed, some appear as being opposite other facets, but rather, the beauty of the diamond is because they "complement" each other. So also, the partaking of "communion" with our Lord has many different ways in which it may be understood and experienced. Many receive communion in somewhat of a ritualistic manner, partaking religiously, rather than first being lifted into the presence of the Lord. There must be a time of preparation for us to truly partake of "communion"with the Lord.

Just as it is not possible for us to "wait on the Lord" or to "worship Him" until wehave passed from the natural into the spiritual realm, it is not possible for us to "receive" the body and blood of the Lord, until we exchange realms. The necessary change is in us, not the bread and fruit of the vine.

The word "communion" has to do with communication. He speaks and we listen. We speak and He listens. Intimate communion is birthed out of intimate relationship and fellowship. Thus, as we enter into communion with Jesus and become "one" with Him,we are able to partake of His very life.

Set Free from the Law of Death

There is foundational principles that are established in the Word of God, which apply to our partaking of communion.

Romans 8:1a- 2
"There is therefore now no condemnation to them which are in Christ Jesus... For the law of the Spirit of Life in Christ Jesus has made me free from the law of sin and death."

This "condemnation" is the judgment (death), which was given to Adam for his transgression (sin). This process of death has been handed down to each of us. We are set free from "the law of sin" through the shed blood of Jesus on the cross. We are set free from "the law of death" through the resurrection of Jesus as a quickening, life-giving spirit.

I Corinthians 15:45
"And so it is written, 'The first man Adam was made a living soul'; the last Adam (Jesus) was made a living (quickening, life-giving) spirit."

Life More Abundantly

Jesus said that He came that we might have life and have that life "more abundantly." This includes divine health and longevity of life. Those who receive this gift of "life" from Jesus will stand out from all others in the quality and length of their life span. Jesus fed the multitude with five loaves and two fishes, but when they became hungry and returned to ask for more, He told them that He had something better for them and said:

John 6:53b
"Except you eat the flesh of the Son of Man, and drink His blood, you have no life in you."

He also said:

John 6:58b
"Your fathers did eat manna and are dead: he that eats of this bread shall live for ever."

John 15:4, 5a
"Abide in Me, and I in you. As the branch cannot bear fruit of itself, except it

abide in the Vine; no more can you, except you abide in Me. I am the Vine, you are the branches."

A branch can only receive its life from the vine; thus, it must be properly connected to the vine. If a strip of bark is totally cut around a tree and removed, the process of death will begin. The tree can no longer receive the life that is drawn up from the root system and will soon die. So also, the life of the "Vine" (Jesus) must flow into us, as being a branch. For this to take place, the branch (us) must be properly connected to the vine. Only then can His life, as the "power of an endless life," flow into our lives.

Hebrews 7:16
"Who is made, not after the law of a carnal commandment, but after the power of an endless life?"

Partake of the Tree of Life on a Regular Basis

Our eating food to sustain our natural body is not an option; rather, it is a necessity. Also, our "partaking" of the life of the Lord is not an option. This partaking of the "body" and "blood" of our Lord must take place more often than partaking of His Life through Communion on the first Sunday of each month. Rather, we must partake on a regular (daily) basis or we will suffer loss, both spiritually and naturally.

After Adam transgressed:

Genesis 3:22
"The Lord God said, 'Behold, the man is become as one of Us, to know good and evil: and now, lest he put forth his hand, and take also of the tree of life, and eat, and live forever.'

I once thought that Adam had eternal existence built within him and would have lived forever if he had not transgressed, but Adam had been formed from dust, which speaks of a created dependency. It is impossible to form anything from dust. It will take the moisture, the very Life of our Lord Jesus Christ — that which flows from the Vine into the branch, for that dust to have form, shape, and purpose. Thus, Adam had to come to the tree of life on a regular basis in order to maintain his life.

"Lest he put forth his hand and take also of the tree of life, and eat, and live forever."

Suddenly, I saw what was being said: when we take communion, we "put forth our hand and take and eat." Adam came regularly and partook, and as a result, he continued to live, but when he transgressed, he was hindered from partaking of the Tree of Life (taking communion), and he began to die.

Had Adam been able to continue to eat, he would have continued to live, but the judgment for transgression was death. Therefore, all the Lord needed to do was to prevent Adam from taking communion (put forth his hand... take... and eat, and live). Therefore, the Lord placed the angel with a flaming sword before the Tree of Life to prevent Adam from partaking.

The Tree of Life is Opened to Us

On the day of Pentecost, this "flaming sword" was removed as a hindrance and become a means of access. It descended and sat upon the head of each of the one-hundred-twenty who were present, as a tongue of fire. It stopped there because it had to be invited to come within. Israel had been offered the "manifest glory" of the Lord and rejected it. Therefore, Jesus is seeking an invitation from us: that He is welcomed in His resurrection glory as a life-giving spirit (tongues of fire), to come within our lives to abide with us.

Revelation 2:7b
"To him that overcomes will I give to eat of the tree of life, which is in the midst of the paradise of God."

As we partake of communion, the way of entrance to the "Tree of Life" is opened to us, and we can partake of His very life, as Jesus is the Tree of Life. When the multitude, which came to see miracles, became hungry, Jesus multiplied five loaves and two fishes, and they were fed to the full **John 6:1-26**.

Later, they came back for more, and when Jesus told them that they were to eat His flesh and drink

His blood, they ridiculed Him and left. He could not, at that time, explain how to partake of His flesh and drink His blood as He had yet to fulfill His preparation to die upon the cross for our sin, and then in resurrection, He become a quickening, life-giving spirit.

When His ministry was completed, the evening before He was to give His life on the cross, Jesus was now able to speak.

I Corinthians 11:23b-25
"He... took bread... and when He had given thanks, He broke it, and said, 'Take, eat: this is My body, which is broken for you: this do in remembrance of Me.' After the same manner also He took the cup, when He had supped, saying, 'This cup is the new testament in My blood: this do you, as often as you drink it, in remembrance of Me.'"

Notice that Jesus said, "This bread is My body, and the cup is My blood." He did not say, "This is an emblem, or symbol of My body and My blood." Then Jesus said that He would not partake again with us, until we partook together with Him, in the Kingdom.

Luke 22:16
"For I say to you, I will not any more eat thereof, until it be fulfilled in the kingdom of God."

The Word says in

Matthew 18:3
"Unless you are converted and become as little children, you will by no means enter the kingdom of heaven"

As we partake of communion, we see bread, but Jesus said, "This is My body." As we partake of the cup, we see the fruit of the vine, but Jesus said, "This is My blood."Having the mind of a child, we simply believe what Jesus said, not what we see.

In Remembrance of Me

The Catholics teach that the "bread" and the "fruit of the vine" must first be transformed into the body and the blood of Jesus. The priest seeks to do this for the believer. Martin Luther said that we can do this for ourselves, without the priest.

However, both are wrong, as we do not need to first "transform" the bread and fruit of the vine. We are to simply believe what Jesus said, and partake of the bread and the fruit of the vine in faith, believing that we are partaking of the body and blood of the Lord.

I Corinthians 11:24-25
"And when He had given thanks, He broke it, and said, Take, eat: this is My body, which is broken for you: this do in remembrance of Me. After the same manner also He took the

cup, when He had supped, saying, This cup is the new testament in My blood: this do you, as often as you drink it, in remembrance of Me." Jesus said that we are to partake "in remembrance of Me." Rather than refer-ring to our remembering His death on the cross, He is directing our thoughts back to the timewhen he told the multitude that they were to "eat His flesh and drink His blood." At thattime, He could not explain how to partake, but now, He can.

With this understanding, when we believe what Jesus said with child-like faith, weare literally partaking of His body and blood. In His resurrection, Jesus became a life-giving Spirit, as He is the Tree of Life.

I Corinthians 15:45 KJV
"And so it is written, 'The first man Adam was made a living soul; the last Adam was made a quickening (living, life-giving) spirit."

Thus, when we partake of communion, we are eating and drinking the very life of the One who is able to impart life. He is a "root" out of dry ground.

Isaiah 53:2a
"For He shall grow up before Him as a tender plant, and as a root out of a dry ground."

Therefore, it can be said that Jesus is the Tree of Life in mystical form, recognizable only to those who have "spiritual" ears and eyes.

I Corinthians 11:28-29
"But let a man examine himself, and so let him eat of that bread and drink of that cup. For he that eats and drinks unworthily, eats and drinks damnation to himself, not discerning the Lord's body. For this cause many are weak and sickly among you, and many sleep."

Life More Abundantly

Communion then is the "mystical form" of the tree of life, hidden from the spiritually blind. Jesus said that if we partake unworthily or partake without understanding that He Himself is the **Tree of Life**, we are merely partaking of the process of death (eats and drinks damnation to himself, not discerning the Lord's body). We are simply receiving bread and the fruit of the vine — another good meal — and we are that much closer to death.

But if we partake with spiritual understanding, knowing what we are doing, we will no longer be weak, sickly, and dying prematurely. Rather, as we rightly partake of communion, we are receiving quickening, life-giving spirit, and we will be living.

I Corinthians 11:26
"For as often as you eat this bread and drink this cup, you do show the Lord's death till He come."

As often as we do this, we are "showing" the Lord's death. This means that we are "demonstrating" the value of it. If we die the same as other people, we are not demonstrating anything. When we partake of **Life**, we are receiving the life that Jesus came to offer: "Life more abundantly."

Paul tells us that we have been set free from "the law of sin and death." As we partake of the bread (His body) and identify with Jesus in His death on the cross, we are forgiven through the blood that He shed on the cross on our behalf. As we identify with the stripes that Jesus bore in His body, we receive healing. Thus, we are partaking "worthily."

We then identify with Jesus through the cup (His blood), as life is in the blood. In His resurrection, Jesus became a "quickening spirit," and in this identification, we are released from the process of death.

I speak to the Lord words, in various forms, include the following:

"Lord, as I receive the bread, I identify with Your body; for in Your body, You bore stripes. And through the blood that flowed from those stripes, I receive healing. You died upon the cross, and in identification with You and the blood You shed in Your death on the cross, I receive forgiveness of sin.

201

"Lord, I partake of the cup, the fruit of the vine, in identification with You, in Your resurrection blood — the power of an endless life. In identification with You as being the Tree of Life, I release my body from the power of death, and I receive longevity of life."

The "Remaining" Ones

As we do this often, we should no longer be sick and dying but living in health and strength.

Just as Adam, we must come to the "Tree of Life" in order to continue to live, or we will progressively die. Therefore, if we understand that communion is the Tree of Life, and then we, in faith, partake of communion as being the Tree of Life, we will live the fullness of the time given us and not die.

The Lord is beginning to reveal the connection between communion and the Tree of Life to those whom He is calling to become "remaining" ones. This is an end-time principle that is being revealed at this present time.

Paul said,

I Thessalonians 4:15b.
"We who are alive and remain at the coming of the Lord..."

Jesus, on the 8th day of His life, was taken into the temple to be dedicated. There were two people there: Anna and Simeon. Anna was old, but Simeon had a "word" that he would not see death until he saw the anointed of the Lord. Anna was "alive," but Simeon was "remaining." Thus, two classes of people were present.

Paul said that in the time of the return of our Lord, these two classes would be present: those who are "alive" through the normal course of life and those "remaining,"whose lives have been extended.

These "remaining ones" are those who, in the time of the return of the Lord, are living beyond their normal span of life. These have learned the principle of communion.They are looking beyond liturgical religious forms into spiritual reality and are partaking in faith, knowing that they are eating the flesh and drinking the blood of Jesus, who is the Tree of Life. And if we partake of the source of Life, Jesus, we will live.

The word says, "as often as you partake." Communion can be taken as often as we desire. If we realize we are partaking of healing and life, we will do so often.

In your daily intimate time with the Lord Jesus Christ, invite the Holy Spirit to speak to you in God's Word. Appropriate what the shed blood of Jesus truly means to you personally from Wade Taylor's preceding teaching. Appropriating the blood means to make it suitable and fitting to apply for daily physical strength and stamina for the course ordained for you to travel. Allow the surging power of this exercise to build, restore, and refresh you for the task set ahead. With wise understanding we can partake of communion daily, which will automatically allow us for daily self examination to bring our transgressions before a Holy God and become transparent in our human fragilities. We must take this exercise seriously and understand the mysteries in communion. As a daily exercise we are establishing the secret of longevity and the restoration of all things.

PRAYER FOR PROTECTION OF HEALTH

Pray this prayer over yourself every day. I suggest taking communion while praying this prayer:

Today I use the wonderful power of the mystery of the shed blood of Jesus for physical protection for my body. I decree divine health in the Name of Jesus Christ. I exercise wisdom and Godly counsel to do all in my power to establish good health practices. I allow the information given to me by Godly sources to educate me and establish me in a healthy lifestyle.

Exodus 15:26
And said, "If you diligently heed the voice of the Lord your God and do what is right in His sight, give ear to His commandments and keep His statues, I will put none of these diseases on you which I have brought on the Egyptians. For I am the Lord who heals you."

I declare and decree that no disease, germs, viruses, tumors, infection, stroke, heart disease, cancer in any form, scoliosis, arthritis, osteoporosis, or incurable disease will come in contact with me or enter my body.

I am redeemed from the curse of the law according to the Word.

Galatians 3:13
Christ has redeemed us from the curse of the law having become a curse for us....

Romans 8:3
For what the law could not do, in that it was weak through the flesh, God did by sending His own Son in the likeness of sinful flesh, on account of sin: He condemned sin in the flesh.

So our physical flesh is being regenerated, cured, healed, repaired, mended and restored to health daily by Jehovah Raphe, my miracle Healer.

Roman 8:11
But if the Spirit of Him who raised Jesus from the dead dwell in you, He who raised Christ from the dead will also give life to your mortal bodies through His Spirit who dwells in you.

Acts 2:24
Whom God raised up, having loosed the pains of death: because it was not possible that He should be held by it.

The same miracles, signs, and wonders will overtake my physical well-being and keep my health in perfect peace and condition.

I will not abuse my body by extremes, but will ask the Holy Spirit to balance the demands on my life with His indwelling Presence. I will take measures to live a sanctified life in regard to what I feed my body that it may provide nourishment and strength. I will exercise wisdom and self-control and restraint from detrimental lifestyles and conditions.

I will learn to pace each day by giving my attention to my Lord and Savior by beginning my day worshipping in His Presence. I will allow reasonable times of physical rest and will retain adequate sleep. I will also commit to moderate exercise so that I may run the race that is set before me.

Proverbs 8: 22,23
The Lord possessed me at the beginning of His way. Before His works of old. I have been established from everlasting, from the beginning, before there was ever an earth.

Proverbs 8:32, 33
Now therefore, listen to me, my children.
For blessed are those who keep my ways.
Hear instruction and be wise and do not
disdain it. For whoever finds me finds life
and obtains favor from the Lord.

Psalm 103:2, 3
Bless the Lord, O my soul; and forget
not all His benefits;
Who forgives all your iniquities, Who
heals all your diseases.

If the stressful influences can't try to undermine your health and peace of mind and try to hinder or rob you of financial victories, then you will remain strong in storms or challenges during adverse situations. If you continue to know the lasting value of communion and apply these daily principles; put at unregenerated thought or influences knowing they are under your feet where they belong by using the power of Gods Word, then you will have no un-fore-seeable violation or transgression over your physical well being, your health, daily stamina, or your endurance.

Boldly decree the protection from Gods word and wisely memorizes this popular and powerful Psalm 91. Most Christians are familiar with this Psalm, but now allow yourself to meditate on it, study it, memorize it, and establish this Word for yourself, your family, and your business, and your business associations. By seeking God in an in-depth word study of this

Psalm you will be able to spiritually own every verse because it will become a living organism for time of need.

It is a desire to see people waking up to the third day authority and an *understanding of the entrance of the third thousand year reign* and the third reformation in place as we have entered into the third millennium. It is a new day! We have transitioned now and overcome and rule in a new spiritual inheritance. As God's people learn how to effectively deal with opposition, they will be able to attain this third inheritance and their assignment of stewarding end-time resources and Kingdom wealth.

Psalm 91:1-16

He who dwells in the secret place of the Most High shall abide under the shadow of the Almighty. I will say of the Lord, "He is my refuge and my fortress; My God, in Him I will trust." Surely He shall deliver you from the snare of the fowler and from the perilous pestilence. He shall cover you with His feathers, and under His wings you shall take refuge; His truth shall be your shield and buckler.

You shall not be afraid of the terror by night, nor of the arrow that flies by day, Nor of the pestilence that walks neither in darkness nor of the destruction that lays waste as noonday.

A thousand may fall at your side and ten thousand at you right hand; but it shall not come near you. Only with your eyes shall you see the reward of the wicked. Because you have made the Lord who is my refuge even the Most High your dwelling place, No evil shall befall you, nor shall any plague come near your dwelling; For He shall give His angels charge over you, to keep you in all your ways. In their hands they shall bear you up, lest you dash your foot against a stone.

You shall tread upon the lion and cobra, the young lion and the serpent you shall trample underfoot. Because he has set his love upon Me, therefore I will deliver him; I will set him on high, because he has known My name. He shall call upon Me, and I will answer him; I will be with him in trouble, I will deliver him and honor him. With long life I will satisfy him and show him My salvation.

Your protection is a settled fact according to Psalm 91 as long as you dwell in the Secret Place of the Most High—that means abiding and dwelling in His presence and on His preceding Word. Make the Lord your true refuge against diseases! Hallelujah! It's settled! You have the victory now!

Have there been inroads or attacks against you? Have you experienced the intrusion of evil influences or assignments coming against your health? Then stand as an over-comer and counter the opposition with the decrees of an over-comer. Do not wait another minute! Render Satan ineffectual by walking in your God ordained authority using the sword of the spirit, which is the Word of God! As you are strengthened with power through the revealed word of God you will remain victorious and rule in all areas pertaining to divine health!

Psalm 41:1-4

Blessed (happy, fortunate, to be envied) is he who considers the poor; the Lord will deliver him in the time of evil and trouble.

The Lord will protect him and keep him alive. He will be blessed in the land; and you will not deliver him to his enemies.

The Lord will sustain, refresh and strengthen him on his bed of languishing. On his bed you (O, Lord) will turn, change, and transform his illness. I said, "Lord, be merciful and gracious to me; heal my inner self for I have sinned against you."

Psalm 41: 8

"An evil disease," say they, "is poured out upon him and cleaves fast to him. And now that he is bedfast he will not rise again."

Psalm 41:10, 11

But you, O Lord be merciful and gracious to me, and raise me up that I might requite them. By this I know that you favor and delight in me, because my enemy does not triumph over me.

No circumstance can come against your health if you won't permit it by standing your ground in Jesus' Name. Immediately stand in agreement with your intercessors and stand firm from the Throne room experience and rise above all strongholds or opposition! The victory has already been won, you have legal authority over that which belongs to you and given from God—you are in a position of Sonship! The joy of the Lord is your strength! Joy unspeakable and full of GLORY! The oil of JOY for the garment of heaviness!

Chapter 11

STRATEGY FOR THE PROTECTION OF MARRIAGES FOR THOSE CALLED TO STEWARD KINGDOM FINANCES

As you pursue God in all your financial endeavors, you must esteem your relationship with your Godly companion—your spouse. The Lord showed me that marriages must be empowered, protected and matured during times of preparation and transition. If you are married, the divine unification of your marriage must be strengthened and shored up because the days ahead are evil. The covenant of marriage is by far the most precious and strongest relationship next to the convent entered into at the time of repentance and salvation with God Himself.

Do you notice how much violence is thrust against Godly unions and holy marriages! Never has there been such an onslaught to demean the very sacredness of the institution of marriage! Our western cultures in nations all over the world now have to face the challenge of the very foundation of the institution of marriage being altered to include and accept same sex marriages as a legal entity!

But in the beginning Gods word clearly punctuates that He hasn't deviated from his original plan. Clearly the human condition has rebelled at the highest levels to tell God that we can lawlessly and falsely make up our own rules! Tolerating deviant lifestyles is a part of the depravity of the human condition that is challenging the *sacredness of the institution of marriage* that we are dealing with in today's society.

We also have seen the fatherless society that has breed co habitation as the norm without the sanctification of a marriage covenant and the brokenness that is perpetuated and the confusion it has wrought when we take a *test run* not knowing that this is not the real deal. It is a false deception that brings trauma, lack of trust, and a lot of baggage to be delivered from in the future!

But we are also very blessed when we hear of the enduring and growing love relationships between couples who have weathered the storms of life but choose to work through all the opposing chaos and celebrate 25, 35 and 50 years of marriage to the same person! This is true wealth and richness that cannot be obtained in materialism and amassed financial successes!

Genesis 2: 18
"Now the Lord God said, It is not good (sufficient, satisfactory) that the man should be alone; I will make him a helper meet (Suitable, adapted, complementary) for him.

Genesis 2:21-25
And the Lord God caused a deep sleep to fall upon Adam; and while he slept, He took one of his ribs or a part of his side and closed up the (place with) flesh. And the rib or part of his side which the Lord had taken from the man He built up and made into woman and He brought her to the man. Then Adam Said, this (creature) is now bone of my bones and flesh of my flesh, she shall be called woman because she was taken out of man. Therefore a man shall leave his father and his mother and shall become united and become one flesh. And the man and his wife were both naked and were not embarrassed or ashamed in each others presence."

Therefore, in your daily time with the Lord, asking Gods opinion of how to strengthen your marriage at this time and shore up and circumvent any oppressive and unresolved conflicts or assignments against the harmony in your marriage. Start by learning to *sanctify* your companion with daily instructions as God reveals to you powerful information from His Word. *Here is a mandate for men* from God. Do you really understand what this scripture means? This scripture says *daily!*

Ephesians 5:26
That He might sanctify and cleanse her [your wife] daily with the washing of the water by the word.

Although this is an exhortation to husbands, the principle holds true that it is important to cover each spouse by decreeing promises from the Word daily over their lives. Exercise this discipline of meditation on these scriptures from the word of God, boldly speaking them as given to you from your study of the Word. Your charge in the Lord is to learn as much spiritual information available to you to protect all areas of your divine union.

The temptations are to keep yourself too busy with business and related assignments to spend the time needed to protect and implement proper covering of your spouse with information given and revealed from the spirit realm. These applications of the Word of God carry a wealth of spiritual weight. It can be easy to become neglectful when balancing busy business routines and schedules, and not focusing on the needs of your spouse, when business transactions and deals demand precious time. It is very important that you establish *good habits* to keep the proper balance, perspective and Godly order of command. This is a challenge in western cultures because of the demands of successful societies climbing corporate structures. These mind sets need to be *mammon proofed* daily. We can easily get caught up in this entire foray and lose the balance when we take our focus off of God.

Here are some helpful 12 strategic points to keep a marriages solidly grounded and respectfully nurtured.

- **Keep God FIRST!**
- **Pray Together!**
- **Respect and honor each other!**
- **Encourage each other to grow together!**
- **Read the Bible together as much as possible!**
- **Be swift to hear & slow to speak!**
- **Make time to communicate with each other!**
- **Protect and honor your marriage vows!**
- **Do not let others come between you and your marriage!**
- **Have a "Mission Statement" for your Marriage & Family!**
- **Thank God everyday for your Mate & the Life you have together!**
- **Understand that "love" is a choice, not a feeling!(You must choose everyday to Love your mate)**

The first order of command daily is to *fall in love with Jesus, the Bridegroom.* Minister your love to Him in spontaneity, joy, and reverential fear.

Offer yourself to the Lord at the beginning of each day as a living sacrifice. Ask Him to create in you a clean heart and to renew a right spirit within you. Yield yourself in total surrender to Him each and every day. This will keep you focused and circumspect.

The second order of command is to be faithful to take inventory and repent of anything needed to God and to your spouse over any unresolved issues or conflicts. Be willing to do so without hesitation. Learn of God, and lean on Him by letting Jesus become a role model of servant-hood to your spouse.

Christian freedom is not the removal of moral restraints; it's the freedom to serve one another. The Gospel of the Kingdom exchanges the oppressive bondage of legalism to become a bond-servant of love.

Galatians 5:13
For you brethren, have been called to liberty; only do not use liberty as an opportunity for the flesh, but through love serve one another.

Galatians 5:16, 17
I say then: Walk in the Spirit, and you shall not fulfill the lust of the flesh. For the flesh lusts against the Spirit, and the Spirit against the flesh; and these are contrary to one another, so that you do not do the things you wish.

Galatians 5:19-21
Now the works of the flesh are evident, which are adultery, fornication, unclean-ness, lewdness, idolatry, sorcery, hatred, contentions, jealousies, outburst of wrath, selfish ambitions, dissentions, heresies, envy, murders, drunkenness, revelings; and the like; of which I tell you beforehand just as I also told you in time past that those who practice such things will not inherit the kingdom of God.

The Bible lists the fruit of the spirit: love, joy, peace, longsuffering, kindness, goodness, faithful-ness, gentleness, self-control. When a believer lives by the fruit of the spirit, no accusation can be brought against them because they are fulfilling the royal law of love. We listed all of these in previous chapters so be sure to review them and apply them as necessary at the leading of our precious Lord.

By you and your companion lovingly serving one another, you are deferring to each other; rendering love to each other. You are offering yourself to gratify the needs and even wants of your companion. It should be a joy to serve each other. Don't you want an uncommon marriage?

By esteeming each other, you are regarding each other more highly and more favorably by offering mutual respect and admiration to each other. You are also putting value to the synergy of a powerful God-ordained union. God put you together to fulfill and strengthen each other to empower the two of you to be ambassadors, recipients and distributors of end-time wealth and kingdom resources.

The strength of your Godly marriage is a threat to the satanic realm or opposing forces of darkness and can come under violent attacks unless you thoughtfully establish the fruit of the spirit in your lives. Your communication with your spouse should help establish the boundaries and needs to come together in harmonious decisions.

Never allow money, the _love of money_, financial success, or the power to amass large sums of money and resources to interfere with your relationship with your marriage partner. Always remember that your focus is on being employed by the CEO of the Universe and you are honorably submitted to His Lordship to steward all of the business entities that He has entrusted to your care. Your wife should be your closest advocate and most devoted and powerful intercessor. She should also be the most powerful alliance to balance and undergurd all of your successes to carry an anointed mantel to increase in wealth.

Proverbs 31:12
"She comforts, encourages and does him <u>*only good*</u> *as long as there is life within her."*

Proverbs 31:11
"The heart of her husband trusts in her confidently and relies on and believes in her securely, so that he has no lack of (honest) gain or need of (dishonest) spoil."

Move your priorities around and watch chaos begin, guaranteed! If you desire a solid marriage, build it on *God's foundation;* constantly study God's wisdom on Christian marriage, the roles of husband and wife, and strengthening your walk with the Lord. This results in a firm foundation for your marriage and life.

Keep God first in your life always! This means remaining faithful to God and His Word. This means diligently seeking to understand and obey the scriptures in ones life. Do you wonder how this works? By walking in constant obedience to God you will have less opportunity to make the "wrong decisions" and "reap" unpleasant side effects in your life. Following Christ does not mean that you never face trials, but rather when trials come into your life you will be equipped to understand and handle them.

Following Christ is not easy though! It is much more than saying you are a Christian. Your life must be an example of Christ's love. If you ever wonder if what you "want" to do is the "Christ's" way, ask yourself this question! Could I see Jesus doing this or acting in this manner?

Psalm 127:1
"Unless the Lord builds the house, they labor in vain who build it."

Proverbs 24:3
"Through wisdom a house is built, And by understanding is established."

Joshua 1:8
"This Book of Law shall not depart from your mouth, but you shall meditate in it day and night, that you may observe to do according to all that is written in it. For then you will make your way prosperous, and then you will have good success."

Colossians 3:1-2
"If then you were raised with Christ, seek those things which are above, where Christ is, sitting at the right hand of God. Set your mind on things above, not on things on the earth."

- Pray, ask God for help. Study the Bible, ponder and disseminate your time of devotion by deeply meditating His expressions personally that are given to you
- Be still (so very important to learn this most valuable discipline)
- Let "bad moods" pass. (These are not times to make or tackle big decisions.)
- Try not to speak in anger. Cool off first. *Words hurt*!
- Take one day at a Time!
- Be good to yourself! Know Jesus loves you!
- If you don't know what to do, do nothing!
- Always be willing to forgive! Some of the most important words in our English Language: *I'm Sorry*

- If you are having relationship problems with your mate, ask yourself...Am I _choosing to "love"_ this person! or am I *choosing* not to love!
- Do you need to put the "eyes of Jesus" on! What do you see?
- Say "I Love You!
- Reach back in your heart to all those "sweet memories" you have with your mate! It's fun to bring them back, then realize just why you picked this person to spend your lifetime with
- Better yet plan new ones!

In order to guard against sexual immorality, God has ordained the sacred relationship of marriage. The concept of an undefiled marriage bed pertains to more than just the approval of a conjugal relationship; it also extends to the married couple's responsibility to preserve their intimacy from the perverse and debasing practices of a lewd society. There is _nothing more powerful in the marriage union_ than a holy and healthy sexual expression to enrich the dynamic of intimacy and connection ordained by God in marriage.

1 Corinthians 7:2-5

Nevertheless, because of sexual immorality, let each man have his own wife, and let each woman have her own husband. Let the husband render to his wife the affection due her, and likewise the wife to her husband. The wife does not have authority over her own body, but the husband does. And like-wise the husband does not have authority over his own body, but the wife does.

Do not deprive one another except with consent for a time, that you may give yourselves to fasting and prayer; and come together again so that Satan does not tempt you because of your lack of self-control.

Hebrews 13:4
Marriage is honorable among all, and the bed undefiled; but fornicators and adul-terers God will judge.

Christian couples should overcome sexual self-ishness and should not deprive one another physi-cally. Three conditions must pertain if sexual activity is to be interrupted in marriage:

1. Mutual consent
2. A limited time
3. For spiritual reasons; not selfish reasons

When we understand Bridal love, we understand romance. Keep romance always in the equation. If conflict comes into the marriage, it is very important to repent and defer to one another, coming back into the perfect will of God by living in harmony with one another.

Psalm 37:8
Cease from anger and forsake wrath; do not fret—it only causes harm..

Ephesians 4:26, 27
"Be angry and do not sin;" do not let the sun go down on your wrath. Nor give place to the devil.

Psalm 4:4, 5
Be angry, and do not sin, meditate within your heart on your bed and be still. Offer the sacrifices of righteousness and put your trust in the Lord.

Go before the Lord and ask Him to help you be the minister of reconciliation. Humility and mercy extended to each other represents the true life of Christ.

1 Corinthians 13:4-7
Love endures long and is patient and kind; love never is envious nor boils over with jealousy, is not boastful or vainglorious, does not display itself haughtily.

It is not conceited (arrogant and inflated with pride); it is not rude (unmannerly) and does not act unbecomingly. Love (God's love in us) does not insist on its own rights or its own way, for it is not self-seeking; it is not touchy or fretful or resentful; it takes no account of the evil done to it [it pays no attention to a suffered wrong]. It does not rejoice at an injustice and unrighteousness, but rejoices when right and truth prevail.

Love bears up under anything and everything that comes, is ever ready to believe the best of every person, its hopes are fadeless under all circumstances, and it endures everything [without weakening]. (Amplified Bible)

Love suffers long. In other words, to demonstrate love is to demonstrate patience. We are all imperfect people. Therefore, we must be patient with each other. Patience is the ability to bear provocation, annoyance, misfortune, or pain without complaint, loss of temper, or anger.

Patience is the ability to suppress restlessness or annoyance when confronted with delay. It's also quiet, steady perseverance; even-tempered care and diligence.

If God demonstrates patience with us, we must be able to exercise patience with our companion as well as all others in our sphere of influence. Paul defines the essence of love and explains the absolute necessity of love.

Since love is non-competitive and non-passive, love actually promotes others to achieve their highest potential. Love does not behave rudely but always displays good manners and courtesy toward others.

God also defines how love is to operate in the role of the wife.

Ephesians 5:22
Wives submit to your own husbands, as to the Lord.

Women were never intended to be inferior to men. However, a wife is specifically called to accept her husband's leadership. Women possess a great strength and ability to support the emotional well-being of the structure of a marriage. That's why it is important to ask the Lord to see your husband through the Lord's eyes.

Husbands and wives both need to affirm each other. Each one of them has different needs; therefore, the affirmation given by a woman to a man is going to be different from the affirmation given from a man to a woman.

Men, for example, are anointed with a God-given gift to protect and provide. Women need to observe this and search for ways to affirm their husbands in his role as provider and protector. Men need to be admired by the wives.

Ephesians 5:23
For the husband is the head of the wife, as also Christ is head of the church; and He is the Savior of the body.
Ephesians 5: 25, 27-29
Husbands love your wives, just as Christ also loved the church and gave Himself for her.... That He might present her to Himself a glorious church, not having spot or wrinkle

or any such thing, but that it should be holy and without blemish.

So husbands ought to love their own wives as their own bodies; he who loves his wife loves himself. For no one ever hated his own flesh, but nourishes and cherishes it, just as the Lord does the church.
Ephesians 5:33

Nevertheless let each one of you in particular so love his own wife as himself, and let the wife see that she respects her husband.

A husband should look to Christ as the divine Bridegroom and follow His pattern of love for the Church. A husband should love his wife sacrificially, listening to her concerns and cares. He should be sensitive to her needs and hurts, just as he cares for the needs of his own physical body and his own well being.

A wife's behavior should reflect that of a chosen bride. As she submits to Christ, she is showing respect and acknowledging her husband. As she responds to her husband's leadership call and his headship over the family, she helps create a relationship designed by God to grow and produce much spiritual fruit.

But by listening and praising him as a true helper, she shows her husband that they are unified in will and purpose. By the grace, power, and the mercy of Christ, this sacred relationship will develop, and they will work together as a spiritual strength and a team for the advancement of the end-times gospel of the kingdom. Safety, protection, and provision for the family are the Godly result of such endeavors.

God divinely appoints couples to work in harmony as teams to execute His work here on the earth. Each companion needs to seek the Lord for the revelation on how to empower and strengthen their relationship. That is the only way they can complete the assignment for which God brought them together. Each couple must realize the strength unity brings, especially so they can fulfill God's plan to work in His financial harvest field.

Referenced here is a list of all scriptures on marriage in the Bible for invoking Gods words for marriage partnerships. These are added for meditating in study and using for decreeing His word for Godly strengthen as an addition for needed spiritual implementation. These will renew couples to serve in ministry assignments in the earth.

Let us call forth this part of our covenant inheritance so that we may run the race with strength and power.

Isaiah 34: 16
"Search from the book of the law, and read: not one of these shall fail; <u>not one shall lack for her mate.</u> For my mouth has commanded it, and his spirit has gathered them"
Isaiah 32: 2
"A man will be as a hiding place from the wind and a cover from the tempest, as

> *rivers of water in a dry place, as the shadow
> of a great rock in a weary land."*

(A man, a husband, a male, and individual person
"ish" portrays maleness and so logically paired with
it's feminine form *"ishah"* –"wife" or woman.)

Husband, Protector, and Provider:

Husbands who open themselves to Gods direction will find both inspiration and power to be those
things for their families; for those attributes of God's
being will flow into and fill their lives.

Genesis 1:27

> *"So God created man in His own image;
> in the image of God He created him; male and
> female He created them. Then God blessed
> them and God said to them, "Be fruitful and
> multiply; fill the earth and subdue it; have
> dominion over the fish of the sea, over the
> birds of the air, and over every living thing
> that moves on the earth."*

Genesis 2: 20-22

> *"But for Adam there was not found a
> helper comparable to him. And the Lord
> caused a deep sleep to fall on Adam, and
> he slept; and He took one of his ribs, and
> closed up the flesh in its place. Then the rib,
> which the Lord God had taken from man He
> made into a woman, and He brought her to
> the man."*

Genesis 2:23

"And Adam said: "this is now bone of my bones and flesh of my flesh; She shall be called Woman, because she was taken out of Man"
Genesis 2: 24-25

"Therefore a man shall leave his father and mother and be joined to his wife, and they shall become one flesh. And they were both naked, the man and his wife, and were not ashamed."
Proverbs 18:22

"He who finds a wife finds a good thing and obtains favor from the Lord."
Proverbs 19:14

"Houses and riches are the inheritance from Fathers, but a wise, understanding and prudent wife is from the Lord."
Proverbs 31:10

"A capable intelligent and virtuous woman who is he who can find her? She is far more precious than jewels and her value is far above rubies or pearls."
Proverbs 12:4

"A virtuous and worthy wife (earnest and strong in character) is a crowning joy to her husband, but she who makes him ashamed is rottenness to the bones."
Proverbs 31:11

"The heart of her husband trusts in her confidently and relies on and believes in her securely, so that he has no lack of (honest) gain or need of (dishonest) spoil."

Proverbs 31:12

"She comforts, encourages and does him ONLY GOOD as long as there is life within her."

Proverbs 31:23

"Her husband is known in the (city's) gates when he sits among the elders of the land." (Amplified Bible)

Proverbs 31:26

"She opens her mouth in skillful and Godly wisdom and on her tongue is the law of kindness (giving counsel and instruction)." (Amplified Bible)

Proverbs 31: 25

"Strength and dignity are her clothing and her position is strong and secure; she rejoices over the future (the latter day or time to come, knowing that she and her family are in readiness for it)!

Proverbs 31:30

"Charm and grace are deceptive, and beauty is vain (because it is not lasting), but a woman who reverently and worshipfully fears the Lord She shall be praised!" (Amplified Bible)

I Corinthians 7: 2

"Nevertheless, because of sexual immorality, let each man have his own wife, and let each woman have her own husband. Let the husband render to his wife the affections due her, and likewise also the wife to her husband."

1 Corinthians 7:3-5

"The husband should give to his wife her conjugal rights (goodwill, kindness, and what is due her as his wife), and likewise the wife to her husband. For the wife does not have (exclusive) authority and control over her own body, but the husband (has his rights); likewise also the husband does not have (exclusive) authority and control over his body, but the wife (has her rights). Do not refuse and deprive and defraud each other (of your due marital rights), except perhaps by mutual consent for a time, so that you may devote yourself unhindered to prayer. But afterwards resume marital relations; lest Satan tempt you (to sin) through your lack of restraint of sexual desire.."

Ephesians 5:23-26

"For the husband is the head of the wife as Christ is the Head of the Church, Himself the Savior of (His) body. As the church is subject to Christ, so let wives also be subject in everything to their husbands. Husbands love your wives, as Christ loved the church and gave Himself up for her. So that He might sanctify her having cleansed her by the washing of water with the Word. "

Ephesians 5:28-29

"Even so husbands love their wives as (being in a sense) their own bodies. He who loves his own wife love himself. For man ever hate his own flesh, but nourishes and

233

carefully protects and cherishes it as Christ does the church."
Ephesians 5:33

"However, let each man of you (without exception) love his wife as (being in a sense his very own self: and let the wife see that she respects and reverences her husband (that she notices him. Regards him. Honors him prefers him venerates and esteems him; and that she defers to him, praises him and loves and admires him exceedingly)." (Amplified Bible)
Ephesians 5:22

"Wives, submit to your own husbands, as to the Lord. For the husband is the head of the wife, as also Christ is head of the Church; and He is the Savior of the body."
Ephesians 5: 24

"Therefore, just as the church is subject to Christ, so let the wives be to their own husbands in everything."
Ephesians 5: 25-26

"Husbands, love your wives, just as Christ also loved the church and gave Himself for her, that He might sanctify and cleanse her with the washing of water by the word that He might present her to Himself a glorious church, not having spot or wrinkle or any such thing, but that she should be holy and without blemish."
Ephesians 5: 28-29

"So husbands ought to love their own wives as their own bodies; he who loves his wife loves himself. For no one ever hated his own flesh, but nourishes and cherishes it, just as the Lord does the church."
Ephesians 5:31

"For this reason a man shall leave his father and mother and be joined to his wife and the two shall become one flesh."
Ephesians 5:33

"Nevertheless let each one of you in particular so love his own wife as himself, and let the wife see that she respects her husband."

A husband looks to Christ the divine Bridegroom a heavenly model for every marriage. His relationship is to love her make sacrifice for her, listen to her concerns, take care of her; be as sensitive to her needs and her hurts as you are to those of our own body.

A wife looks to be the chosen Bride of Christ. In this she behaves toward her husband by respecting him, acknowledging his calling as "head" of the family, responds to his leadership, listens to him, praises him, she is unified in purpose and will with him; and is a true helper.

This can only be done by willpower or resolve. Because we are Gods workmanship He will bring this about.
1 Peter 3:2

"When they observe the pure and modest way in which you conduct yourselves, together with our reverence (for your husband: you are to feel for him all that reverence includes, to respect, to defer to, reverence him, to honor, esteem appreciate, prize and in the human sense to adore him, that is to admire, praise be devoted, to deeply love and enjoy your husband)."
1 Peter 3:5-6

"But let the inward adorning and beauty of the hidden person of the heart, with the incorruptible and unfading charm of a gentle and peaceful spirit which (is not anxious or wrought up, but) is very precious in the sight of God. For it was thus that the pious women of old who hoped in God were (accustomed to beautify themselves and were submissive t their husbands adapting themselves to them as themselves secondary and dependant up on them)."
Malachi 2:16

"For the Lord the God of Israel says:" I hate divorce and marital separation and him who covers his garment (his wife) with violence. Therefore keep a WATCH upon your spirit (that it may be controlled by My Spirit) that you deal not treacherously and faithlessly with your marriage mate."

The Lord is bringing together His choice in partnerships. We must leave behind that which we have experienced, and

*press forward to that which He has prom-
ised and provided. God is giving treasures,
jewels, gifts to enhance and adorn each
other respectively. Let us protect the jewels,
let us esteem and honor these treasures in
each other that we have been entrusted with.*
**People have been trained and prepared
for this hour to serve in God's end-time
army. Now let us receive the gifts of God to
complete our assignments in the earth and
get the job done.**
James 1:17

*"Every good gift and every perfect gift
is from above, and comes down from the
Father of lights, with whom there is no vari-
ation or shadow of turning."*

THE MEANING OF THESE WORDS:

GOOD: Good in a physical and moral sense, and
which produces benefits, the word is used of persons,
things, acts, conditions and so on. A synonym of
"agathos" is "kalos", good in an aesthetic sense,
suggesting attractiveness, excellence.

PERFECT: Refers to that which has reached an end,
It means to finished or completed, perfect. Applying
it to persons it signifies consummate soundness, and
includes the idea of being whole. In application to
believers it denotes MATURITY.

ESTEEM: The word means to regard highly or favorable. It also means regarded with respect or admiration. To consider as a certain value or type. A favorable opinion or judgment, respect or regard estimation or value.

VALUE: This word means relative worth or importance. The abstract concept of what is right or worthwhile a desirable principle, or standard. Consider with respect the worth or importance to regard highly, to esteem. It is the estimated or assigned worth magnitude or quality.

Chapter 12

JESUS, I TRUST YOU WITH MY DAUGHTER

This word *"trust"* encompasses the all-consuming dependence and hope to extend ourselves to Jesus in those areas where we see slow progress and are seeking to have an encouraging outcome. When we don't have all the answers; when there's been a cloud of separation, and that glimmer we've yearned to see somehow doesn't ignite explosively on our timetable—that's just when we need to trust Jesus.

As I prepared to write this last chapter of the book, I knew that I couldn't leave out children, our most precious commodity.

Psalm 127: 3-5 states:
"Behold children are a heritage from the Lord, The fruit of the womb is a reward,
Like arrows in the hand of a warrior,
So are the children of one's youth.

Happy is the man who has his quiver full of them; They shall not be ashamed, But shall speak with their enemies at the gate."

As we define trust, few see that it is a reliance on the integrity, strength, or ability of a person so that we may have a confident expectation or hope for something we desire to see changed; and a break-through for the final outcome. Trust stretches us to retain this confidence and reliance on God, the one upon whom we rely with a heartfelt peace that He is working tirelessly on our behalf. The word *trust* establishes our expectation in *someone who can be entrusted* with all that is needed to be released. It is a means of building our faith in His governance with a belief in *trusting* it is His responsibility. This is how we place complete confidence and authority in Him alone. This truly puts us to rest.

Proverbs 3:5
Trust in the Lord with all your heart, and lean not on your own understanding.

When we think of children we look at them as our descendants and our legacy. As part of our direct ancestry they are called to be our heirs, and they will be entrusted with any fortune that we may incur in this lifetime be it spiritual or monetary. To love and serve our offspring as good role models is one of the ways that we may prosper. I feel that this chapter was so necessary to remind us that no matter the condition of our families, God has a plan of redemptive prosperity. This prosperity is not tied up in tangible things, but in priceless treasures called our children, and eventually our grandchildren. Our generations coming up are part of the spiritual and physical prosperity promised to us. We have this assurance from God, because He can redeem the time that has been stolen. He can redeem our inheritance.

Proverbs 13:22
"A good man leaves an inheritance to his children's children, but the wealth of the wicked is <u>stored up for the righteous."</u>

Through lack of maturity or responsible training there may be some question marks in our hearts to be cast over upon the Lord. Our understanding is limited, contained, and small in scope! God's plan is vast, huge, and displayed to bring glory to His Name.

Proverbs 30:5
Every word of God is pure; He is a shield to those who put their trust in Him.

When we talk about God's plan of prosperity, we must put monetary wealth in perspective. I feel the example of the greatest wealth any parent could ever have is the love, respect, and admiration of their children. That is the truest form of prosperity indeed!

For that reason I want to take some time to tell you a little about myself and my family (which consists of me and my now adult daughter Desdemona). I was divorced early in my brief marriage. So I was a single parent. As God began to train me through seasons of seeking Him, He had to get my priorities about true wealth or that which is true prosperity into perspective. The word prosperity means a successful, flourishing or thriving condition. I had a lot of work to do in the area of my relationship with my daughter. We were anything but "prosperous" in our relationship by Gods standards. Desdemona is a beautiful, brilliant young woman. She is a special daughter with tremendous giftings and talents.

Children are amazing treasures entrusted to us. Without strong and deeply rooted parenting skills based on Christian values, good training and the Word of God, we are somewhat undone about how to train our children for what lies ahead. As a single parent I was greatly lacking in proper parenting skills, being unaware and clueless because of the demands and the conditions of our lives. I didn't have the time necessary to devote to the things of God in a way that would have circumvented much difficulty. If I had known how to seek God diligently at this time, I would have walked in a level of maturity that would have circumvented much, but I do believe that we can learn to assist others on the journey through our "on the job" training as we move forward.

This did not become relevant for me as a single mother while my own daughter was very young. But as I pursued God years later I began to see with the eyes of God. She was a girl who did not know her Father's love. There is presently a great move of the spirit of God to bring much restoration to pass. God is restoring the "Father Heart of God" to abandoned and bruised and isolated humanity. We are hearing this more and more as we cry out "Abba Father." This has been a fatherless generation and God is taking up individual causes!

As we breezed through the years, we encountered seasons of joy, delight, and, yes, much confusion, conflict and turmoil. We typified the fragmented single family of this generation. I was a mother who operated in a momentum of striving, stretched to the max by the demands of life, not strong in knowing how to rest in God's provision. Yes, God performed many supernatural wonders and wrought many miracle provisions in spite of my ineptness. But God's best is definitely a family with two parents. We see the effects of Fatherless children on our society and in every culture today. In western nations there is a diabolical onslaught on children and youth on many levels.

Actually it is of global proportions the circumstances are just changed! We deal with materialism, mammon and the debauched choice of this culture. Other nations deal with poverty, homelessness, disease, and being orphaned. Children are our future and our hope. There has been so much suffering! But God is taking up these causes world wide!

Our greatest desire as parents is to know that we did everything perfectly for our children. Even so, it is hard to carry that responsibility. Sooner or later we come to a place where the veil is lifted off of our understanding, and we see the places where we've missed the mark. When this happens, we need to come to God in humility and repentance and pull on everything He has available to us to reorder our lives.

In the last several years as God has prepared me to go forth, my greatest hearts cry has been to see my daughter at the level of discernment and dedication to the talents within her; and to walk into the things God has designed for her to do. I've asked the Lord to show me how to see things as she sees them; to feel as she feels, so that I know how to pray for her properly at each juncture.

I asked Jesus for mercy, and as the Lord revealed to me the many places where I have missed the mark many, many times by being imperfect and unskilled. Through prayer and asking God how my daughter saw things, I began to see things through my daughter's eyes. There were places of pain, rejection, disrespect, lack of patience, and so on. She felt unprotected and it was a heart wrenching reality when God began to show me her thoughts!

Yes, there were good things too, fun memories, but God must show us all the truth so that we can pray for restoration. Many of us have been living in a society that demands such intense scheduling which has kept us so busy making a living; being as successful as possible in our endeavors, and establishing a form of prosperity so that we have ended up neglecting our families. As we experienced the tragedy of September 11, 2001 we began to see people look at their priorities a lot differently. Suddenly family was a more important priority, and surely we have learned much from that fateful day on what our priorities should be.

Somehow there has been an illusion as to what God's perfect plan really is for our lives. What is true prosperity? The Word tells us in *3 John 2: "Beloved, I pray that you may prosper in all things and be in health, just as your soul prospers.*

The soul consists of the mind, will, and emotions. And it is in our souls that many of us need to be redeemed from "soulish carnality" and mindsets. We need to step into the realm of the spirit with new discernment, thus operating out of our "spirit man" instead of out of our natural, unregenerated, carnal nature. God's redemptive judgments establish a new perspective and direction.

When we operate with spiritual discernment and not soulishly it gives us a whole new dimension of revelational insights for our lives. The illusions and concepts once clouded are transformed into the mind of Christ—thinking God's thoughts. We will literally transition into a deeper understanding and expression of life's purposes as we operate out of our spirit instead of our carnal nature.

As we spend more time disciplining ourselves to live in intimate relationship with the Lord, our ability to see things from a spiritual perspective is heightened. A flow is established and we become encouraged by our progress. In this way we become better parents.

It's obvious that we only go through our children's growing up years once. We don't get a rerun; this is not a test session. If we can take our ineptness, our mistakes and failures and use them to help educate future generations, we will still have succeeded.

But how do we take weak parenting skills and perfect them so we can redeem the time?

The first place we need to go is to our knees for direction. As I continued to see a breach between me and my now grown daughter, I knew I had to get a revelation from God how to mend this relationship. Before God could distribute a level of stewardship of His kingdom resources through me, my own family situation had to be in order. My assignment was to redeem the precious time and redefine the relationship with my now adult daughter.

As God showed me some of my mistakes, I began to ask Him for forgiveness and His mercy. I then began to wonder how God could turn things around? He began to show me a perspective and a view that I had never seen before. It was an unveiling of years of deception and ungodly order. It was a view that crushed my spirit, but God pulled back the curtain in my understanding so that I could see clearly. I needed to have a new form of ability to communicate with my daughter. He had to teach me that my responses to her—regardless of the situation—needed to always be calm and collected. I was reactionary in the past because of many responsibilities.

For example, if something were spoken through my daughter in the past provoked an emotional response, God taught me how to just smile sweetly and pray under my breath, *"Jesus, I trust you with my daughter. Jesus, You know what she needs."*

I also knew the most important expression of love would be to tell her "I am sorry," and ask her forgiveness in areas where I fell short.

I believe many young adults are robbed of a better life because of our poor parenting skills. Many children have working parents. In fact, in the last several decades, gaining money and possessions played a huge roll in how we managed our lives. Christians are guilty as well! How that paradigm has changed in our world as we have been shocked into the reality of a world in turmoil.

God wants us successful, but not at the expense of our children. Our priorities must be balanced and in the right perspective. We need to be worshippers of God first, devoted to our family second, and then tremendous business success will follow supernaturally by the hand of God at the appointed time.

Those things that rob us of our focus on God, our family, and our business—all the time robbers—must be circumcised out of our lives, and the proper balance put back in. Children need our time, not just heaped up things and material rewards.

If we give ourselves to our children, we produce gifts to bless this world because our children will ultimately go back out into society to lead, direct, and serve a hurting world.

I learned a great lesson while I was a Bible College student. A dynamic young man led prayer everyday, and he often spoke of his mother with affection. She was the one who prayed him into the Kingdom of God. He had been in jail and gangs before he had come to the Lord, but always carried an anointed evangelistic call on his life.

This young man also taught a class, "The Authority of the Believer," and every time he made a statement apropos to praying over my daughter, I highlighted it in my notes and wrote my daughter's name next to it.

You see, God sees our desires and our faithfulness, and He acknowledges our prayers. Our heart-cries are His heart-cries.

While still in school, it was my custom to get up everyday at 4:00 a.m. to pray for one hour before the day began. I would go downstairs and sit on a little heart-shaped, braided mat, using the light above the stove so I could see. This is where I prayed each morning. I would call out everything on this prayer list and confirm, declare and prophesy scriptures over my daughter.

Below is the first prayer I developed for my daughter. It has encouraged many, and I hope it will encourage you. There is hope in prayer. God has a plan to make you wealthy on all levels, but with your children it must start with a wealth of communication and interaction first.

A PRAYER FOR CHILDREN

I pray divine structure to _____'s emotions and his/ her thoughts.

Satan, in the Presence of Jesus I rebuke you from __ ____. I bind you and I break your power in Jesus' Name.

I pray for _____ to break through and get his/her spirit connected with God's Spirit.

I pray all doors are closed so the devil cannot make an entrance into _____'s life.

I pray that _____ knows who he/she is in Christ.

I plead the blood of Jesus over the environment that covers and controls _____.

I pray that _____ is repulsed by the powers of darkness.

_____ lives strong in the Spirit and builds a resistance to the power of the devil.

I pray that _____ cooperates with the Holy Spirit.

_____ comes into agreement with Your divine destiny.

_____'s only joy or hope is through the door of Jesus.

I pray that *You* remove all relationships out of _____ 's life not birthed by the Holy Sprit! Those not in line with Your will.

_____ has no joy in the lust of the eyes, the lust of the flesh, and pride of life.

_____ has wisdom and guidance and a teachable spirit.

I call _____ out of the worlds system into the high call.

_____, your future and hope is in God. When you make the decision for God, He will take over. Then He will lead you in life.

_____ is not his/her own. _____ is bought with a price and glorifies God in his/her body.

The words of _____'s mouth and meditations of his/her heart are acceptable in the sight of the Lord.

_____ will not be denied what God has ordained him/her to have.

_____ knows the will of God by living a sanctified life.

_____, you don't represent yourself; you represent a generation.

_____ will provide his/her highest call in the Holy Spirit.

_____ walks in the power and anointing of the call.

SCRIPTUAL PRAYER FOR CHILDREN

Insert your children's name(s) into these key places in the following scripture:

Isaiah 43:3-6
"But now (in spite of past judgments for ___
_____sins, thus says the Lord, He who created you_____, and He who formed you, _____
_____Fear not for I have redeemed you ____
_____ (ransomed you by paying a price instead of leaving you captives _____); I have called you by your name_____ you are mine."

Proverbs 1:3-5
"_____Receive the instruction and wise dealing and the discipline of wise thoughtfulness righteousness justice and integrity, That prudence may be given to _____and knowledge and discretion and discernment to the youth. _____, a wise man/woman will hear and increase learning, and ___

_____a person of understanding will acquire skill and attain to sound counsel (so that he may be able to steer his course rightly."

Romans 8: 20-22

"For the creation (nature) _____ was subjected to frailty (futility, condemned to frustration), not because of some intentional fault on its part, but by the will of Him Who so subjected it-yet with hope (for)_____. The nature (creation) _____ will be set free from its bondage to decay and corruption and_____ (will) gain an entrance into the glorious freedom of Gods children. We know that the whole creation_____ (of irrational creatures) has been moaning (groaning) together in the pains of labor until now."

Isaiah 41:11-12

"Behold, all those who were enraged and enflamed against _____ shall be put to shame and confounded; they shall be as nothing, and they shall perish. _____ shall seek those who contended with _____but you shall not find them; they who war against _____ shall be as nothing, as nothing at all."

Isaiah 43:3-6

"For I am the Lord your God, the Holy One of Israel, your Savior; I gave Egypt for _____'s ransom, Ethiopia and Seba in exchange (for _____ _'s release) because.

_____ is precious in my sight and honored and because I love _____; therefore, I will give men in return for you, and people for your life. Fear not, for I am with you; I will bring _____'s descendants from the east, and gather them from the west; I will say to the north, 'Give up!' and to the south, 'Keep not back!" Bring My sons from afar and My daughters from the ends of the earth."

Isaiah 42:12-13

"Let _____ give glory to the Lord, and declare His praise in the islands and the coastal regions. The Lord shall go forth like a mighty man; He will rouse up His zealous indignation and vengeance like a warrior (on behalf of) _____ He shall cry out, yes, shout aloud, He will do mightily against His enemies." (on behalf of)_____

2 Corinthians 6:2

"For He says, 'In a time of favor (of an assured welcome) I have listened to and heeded _____'s call, and I helped _____on the day of deliverance (the day of salvation) Behold, now is truly the time for a gracious welcome, and acceptance (of you from God) behold, now is the day of_____'s salvation!"

Proverbs 1:8

"_____, hear the instruction of your father, and do not forsake the laws of your mother."

Psalm 138:7-8

"Though _____ walks in the midst of trouble, You will revive _____; You will stretch out Your hand against the wrath of _____'s enemies, and Your right hand will save _____. The Lord will perfect that which concerns _____; Your mercy, O Lord, endures forever; forsake not the works of Your hands."

Isaiah 53:11

"He shall see the travail of His soul, and be satisfied. By His knowledge My righteous Servant_____ shall justify many, for He shall bear_____'s iniquities."

Romans 4:17

"... in the presence of Him who _____ believed, even God, who gives life to the dead_____ and calls those things which do not exist as though they did."

Ephesians 1:16-19

"I do not cease to give thanks for _____, making mention of _____ in my prayers: (For I always pray to) the God of our Lord Jesus Christ, the Father of glory, that He may grant_____ a spirit of wisdom and revelation (of insight into mysteries and secrets) in the (deep and intimate) knowledge of Him. By having the eyes of _____'s heart flooded with light, so that you can know and understand the hope to which He has called you, and how rich is His glorious inheritance in the saints, (His set apart

ones) And (so that _____ can know and understand) what is the immeasurable and unlimited and
surpassing greatness of His power in and for us who
believe toward us who believe, as demonstrations in
the working of His mighty strength."

Proverbs 1: 3-5

"_____ receive (s) instruction in wise
dealing and the discipline of wise thoughtfulness,
righteousness, justice and integrity. That prudence
may be given to the simple_____and knowledge
to the youth_____. The wise_____also
hear and increase in learning, and _____the
person of understanding will acquire skill and attain
to sound counsel (so that _____he/she may be
able to steer his course rightly."

Jeremiah 20:11-12

"But the Lord is with _____ as a mighty and
terrible one; therefore _____'s persecutors will
stumble, and will not overcome _____. They will
utterly be put to shame, for they will not deal wisely
or prosper (in their schemes); their eternal dishonor
will never be forgotten. But, O Lord of hosts, You
who try the righteous, who see the heart and the
mind, let _____ see Your vengeance on them; for
to you have I revealed and committed my cause."

In my second year of Bible College, I prepared a
thesis on angels. While preparing this paper, I began
to pray Daniel 10:11-12 over myself, inserting my

own name in strategic places. For example, I prayed this scripture as follows:

"And the angel said to me, "O [Ann], you greatly beloved [woman] understand these words I speak to you and stand upright for to you I am now sent." And while He was saying this I stood up trembling. Then He said, "Fear not, [Ann], for from the first day that you set your heart and mind to understand and humble yourself before your God, YOUR WORDS WERE HEARD and I HAVE COME AS A CONSEQUENCE OF (AND IN RESPONSE TO) YOUR WORDS! "Daniel 10:11-12 (Amplified Bible).

Hallelujah! What power is released in decreeing this scripture over ourselves and our children.

Daniel 10:13
...Then Michael, one of the chief [of the celestial] princes came to help me.

The angels, the chief archangel, harkened to the voice of Daniel's words! The angels are empowered in battle to do the will of God as we proclaim God's Word over our children and *loved ones*!

In the second year of Bible College in the second month, I received a post card from my daughter with the picture of an angel on it. She stated on the card, "Mom, I saw this post card, and thought of you. You're my angel. I'm on an 'angel' kick. Get me something with angels on it."

I felt this was God's encouragement for my prayers that had been going forth. My daughter was that I was writing a thesis on angels at that ...t the Lord knows just how to show us He's ...g behind the scenes.

As I have applied the Word of God, I've seen tremendous in-roads in the way my daughter and I connect and relate to each other. God is on the move to turn old hurts, wounds, strongholds and miscommunications around. He is a faithful God.

Our children need to be affirmed by their Heavenly Father, but if they don't know their earthly father's love, they will undoubtedly have areas that need to be healed. For example, the Lord allowed me to minister to a man a few years ago who had never been affirmed by His father.

The Lord gave me this dream about him. The Lord told me this man's middle name in the dream, and I saw him looking at a small child or boy. Somehow he himself was a part of this small child, and I saw great internal turmoil and conflict within the man.

When I called this man, I asked him who did the name belong to that I had gotten in the dream, I had to step out in faith with what I had been given. He told me it was his middle name just as the Lord gave it to me in the dream. Of course, I had no way of knowing this man's middle name, except by revelation from God.

I learned that when he was fourteen years old, he wished his father would die. He actually said to God," kill my father!" Three days later, his father died. What a tragic experience for a young man! You see, he had never been affirmed by a loving father, and he no doubt suffered years of tremendous guilt over his father's death.

Without affirmation, especially from an earthly father, we have a hard time accepting our Heavenly Father's love. Without that love we don't know how to develop proper intimacy with God, and without an intimate relationship with God we won't experience a relationship with God.

Fathers need to cultivate a loving relationship with their children, because we must experience that love to relate properly with their Heavenly Father. Children *need the affirmation of their father's love to develop spiritually!*

The word "affirm" *comes* to me many times. The word "affirm" means to conform or ratify; to express agreement with; to uphold, or support. People have not *always* been properly affirmed as they grow up. Without proper affirmation, *kids grow up with a distorted sense of who they are.*

The Lord told me that many people don't know the Father's love. We can experience the anointing; we can sense His Presence, but some of us have never felt His love overwhelm us, giving us new confidence and security. This often occurs when "Daddy's" love was not experienced in every area, resulting in an area of emotional deprivation.

God's love must be experienced by revelation. It has to come by personal experience. As "Daddy" says, come here and sit on my lap, his big secure arms holding *us* and wrapping us in an embrace of protection and peace, we feel a resident ability to abandon ourselves and totally entrust ourselves to Him.

As we comprehend this love, security, and protection from our heavenly Father, we step into the confidence and affirmation *God* always ordained for us to experience. Then we can begin to seek the place of comfort that can only be received from *God*.

This experience of unconditional love can heal us from the loss, pain, rejection, bruises, hurts, wounds and all other personal lacks. In God's Presence, He continues to pull us to Him, embracing and loving us, giving us His approval and confirmation.

I believe as God's children begin to step into His all-consuming love, we will receive the completeness we have lacked in our other relationships, thus preparing us to excel in all our endeavors. As our sense of purpose becomes sharper, we no longer strive, but we rest in God's resident power, allowing God's grace in all that we do. Our discernment sharpens and our ability to hear His specific directives is clarified. I trust God that this will minister Spirit and life to you.

Fathers must be prayer warriors also. This is not just a woman's responsibility. The Bible supports this:

Luke 18:1
Then He spoke a parable to them that MEN always ought to pray and not lose heart.

True humility in prayer is not gender-bound. For example, we need to allow our prayers and relationships to be modeled after the lives of Moses,

Abraham, David, and Paul—true men of humility, stature, and prayer. Our children need godly fathers.

I would like to close this chapter with a poem I wrote about fathers.

Where Are My Fathers?

Where are all my mighty men—my fathers,
my strong ones?
Have you abdicated your position in the land
because of your wounds, hurts and especially pride?
I've bought you with blood by a violent
death and shame to cover your nakedness.

You have perverted your anointed, God-
given position.
Your children have been abandoned, lost to
the wolves of a debauched society.
And the pain still burns in your soul.
The little ones are wounded.
They are held in strangulation and
strongholds,
with inner turmoil and conflict, and no spiritual rudder.
They churn with yearning to have liberty,
and to be set free to be who they are called
to be.

It's a war of the spirit world to deafen their
ears and darken their eyes from the wooing
of His Holy Spirit.

Oh fathers, turn your hardened hearts.
Cry out for mercy!
Let your souls travail! Repent!

Oh, Holy Father, the Father of all fathers,
touch the men and bring them in.
Let them take up their position of spiritual
authority.
Let them cover their families.
Pray, fathers, pray. Pray, fathers, pray.
Don't take the burden away until our fathers
learn to pray.

BIBLIOGRAPHY

FACE TO FACESong written and produced by Kim
Clement of Prophetic Images Ministry. Copyright ©
registered February 25, 1998. Used with permission.

THE LASTING VALUE OF COMMUNION
Written by Wade E. Taylor of Wade Taylor
Ministries
wetbanner@aol.com http://www.wadetaylor.org/
Used with permission.

THE WATCH OF THE LORD Three Stranded Cord
Strategic Ministries, Sue and Fred Rowe, Kern Region
Prayer Watch, California. pryrwatch@sbcglobal.net.
Used with Permission.

SPIRIT FILLED LIFE BIBLE
Copyright © 1991 by Thomas Nelson, Inc.
The Holy Bible, The New King James Bible printed
in the United States of America

FRIENDS OF THE BRIDEGROOM
Training Manual www.fot.com
Song of Songs Mike Bickel

DON'T JUST STAND THERE, PRAY SOMETHING
Authored by Ronald Dunn copyright 1992 Thomas Nelson Publisher Nashville, Tenn.

15 POINT THESIS http://www.simsonwolfgang.de
Wolfgang Simson: He was born in (1959) functions as a strategy consultant, researcher, theologian and journalist within various networks and regional and global strategy think tanks.

Footnotes taken from the book of Ephesians page 1796 chapter 6:12 quotes used in part to describe spiritual warfare. Spirit Filled Life Bible

Quote on Marriage Tips from www.geocities.com/
Heartland/plains/8218/marriage.html

CPSIA information can be obtained at www.ICGtesting.com
Printed in the USA
LVOW040123100412

276849LV00001B/1/P